THE ACCIDENTAL GARDEN

ALSO BY RICHARD MABEY

Food for Free

The Unofficial Countryside

The Common Ground

The Flowering of Britain (with Tony Evans)

The Frampton Flora

Gilbert White

Home Country

Whistling in the Dark, In Pursuit of the Nightingale

Flora Britannica

Nature Cure

Beechcombings

The Full English Cassoulet

A Brush with Nature

Weeds

The Perfumier and the Stinkhorn

Turned Out Nice Again

Dreams of the Good Life

The Cabaret of Plants

Turning the Boat for Home

THE ACCIDENTAL GARDEN

GARDENS, WILDERNESS AND
THE SPACE IN BETWEEN

RICHARD MABEY

Profile Books

First published in Great Britain in 2024 by
Profile Books Ltd
29 Cloth Fair
London
ECIA 7JQ
www.profilebooks.com

Copyright © Richard Mabey, 2024

1 3 5 7 9 10 8 6 4 2

Typeset in Dante by MacGuru Ltd
Printed and bound in Great Britain by Clays Ltd, Elcograf S.p.A.

The moral right of the author has been asserted.

A CIP catalogue record for this book is available from the British Library.

ISBN 978 1 80522 070 1
eISBN 978 1 80522 071 8

FSC
www.fsc.org
MIX
Paper | Supporting
responsible forestry
FSC® C018072

For Polly

Contents

1

A SEA OF GRASS

The poet R. S. Thomas once described that most commodious of institutions, the garden, as 'a gesture against the wild/The ungovernable sea of grass'. Which sounds pretty much like a summary of the whole human project on planet Earth. We still struggle to find a gesture in our relations with the natural world which is more like a handshake than a clenched fist.

My childhood garden was separated from an ungovernable sea of grass by a single strand of barbed wire. On one side was my dad's neat and productive plot, with its box hedges and dahlias and asparagus beds. On the other, fast returning to the wild, lay the abandoned grounds of Berkhamsted Hall, the seat of Graham Greene's Uncle Charles. We local kids used it as our playground, and called it The Field, as if it were the only one.

But the wire didn't mark a sharp separation of wild and cultivated growth, straight lines versus billows, high-born apples against crabs. The grounds of the demolished hall – fifty acres of tousled grass and stately trees – still held traces of what had been there before, like archaeological relics. It was dotted with grassed-over tennis courts and terraces and choked-up wells. The debris of the building was laid out in long brick tumuli. Our local gang inhabited this ghostly plot like indigenous people. We mapped out sacred meeting places, built a camp in the root hole of a storm-felled chestnut tree, stamped out tracks for soapbox carts, munched young hawthorn leaves and scrumped walnuts. Forty years earlier, the young Graham Greene had sat in his eyrie on the hall's roof, gazed out over the expansive grounds and dreamed of being an explorer – but we imagined we were doing it for real.

Our garden had feral accents of its own. Dad had built an elegantly curved rose terrace out of the metal tubes from our Second World War Anderson bomb shelter. His home-made greenhouse incorporated bricks and marble slabs looted from the hall's ruins. Turves from the one-time tennis courts found their way into several lawns. And one summer holiday I plundered Dad's root vegetables to sell on a stall I'd set up on the track along which commuters trudged up from the station towards that wire fence and home. Each territory fed the other with resources and ideas.

I feel as if I've been shuttling back and forth across that wire all my life. I've been drawn by the fusions we've made between nature and culture, especially in language and landscape. And then cheered every time the natural world cocks a snook at our hubris and goes its own way. Rarer to find are moments of a middle way, of cohabitation rather than manipulation. It would be glib to suggest that the immeasurably complex problems of a whole world are mirrored in the small confrontations and challenges of the garden. But maybe the mindset needed for both is the same: the generosity to reset the power balance between ourselves and the natural world.

It was late in my life before I had a garden to call my own. I'd left Berkhamsted after a long illness in 2002, and my partner Polly and I moved into our patch of earth in south Norfolk the following year, elated by the novelty and hopefulness of a late-in-life romance. I'd spent sixty years among the woods and downs of the Chilterns, she among the broads and marshes of Norfolk. We were, in our environmental backgrounds, like chalk and cheese. We'd acquired a late sixteenth-century timber-framed farmhouse set in about two acres of conventional flower and vegetable beds and a tangled mosaic of grass, trees and water. By our standards it was a small estate, and we were thrilled by the challenges it offered. Could Polly and I – compulsive intuitive grower and instinctive hands-off rewilder respectively – find a common modus operandi? Happily we shared Gerard Manley Hopkins's disquiet at 'what would the world be, once bereft / Of wet and of wildness? Let them be left'. But in two acres? Was there room for both the weeds and the wilderness *and* the defining human habit of pottering?

Gardens aren't quite like other human spaces. They're borderlands, possessed, designed and controlled by one species, but occupied by myriads more. Some have been introduced by the notional gardener, some arrived as spontaneous visitors, many settled in as freeholders before the house was built, all with their own lives to lead. The echoes of these pasts linger. Every April, in a small patch of our border between the sweet williams and the soap-wort a mysterious odour floats up from the ground. It's elusive, musky, reminiscent of fox – except that this is one animal we've never seen in the garden. What it most reminds me of is the powerful aroma of Crown Imperial, the majestic fritillary which flowers at this moment in the spring. But no Crown Imperial grows here or nearby. Nor has scrabbling through the soil exposed any submerged relics of the bulb, which can whiff as foxily as the flower. This is fertile ground for fancies. Did *Fritillaria imperialis* grow here once, and leave some kind of aromatic ghost in the soil, rekindled in the plant's flowering time? Did foxes steal invisibly in when we were abed?

The sense of some obstinate living infrastructure, adapting or indifferent to human changes, has been power-ful. Even the house itself feels like a momentary carapace over an anciently established community. Wrens nest in the thatch just feet from the bedroom window. Pipistrelle and long-eared bats roost in the loft. Every summer, black ants swarm through the floor of the library from some invisible underground fortress. In two successive Junes I've surprised juvenile treecreepers perched on my com-puter monitor, as if it were simply some extension of the outside branchwork. My late friend Ronald Blythe, who lived in a similarly ancient farmhouse in the Stour Valley, wrote: 'I have always been conscious of residents other than humanity who give this address and whose claim for shelter is historic.'

The commonly understood definition of a garden is

less generous. It's an arena for the display of the gardeners' tastes and ideas, and their mastery, or at least paternal stewardship, of nature. When you step back a little, it's chastening to realise the degree of unquestioned license that possession of a garden gives. Over this finite patch of a finite planet you can do just about whatever you like – trash it, cover it with Astroturf or decking, craft it into an Impressionist masterpiece or a workaday food lot. Whether you come armed with weedkiller or a charitable bug-hostel, you are in dominion over all the garden's other citizens. If this was a human community, we would call it colonialism.

But of course we can't admit this. Regardless of any green or de-colonising aspirations, we are irrevocably in charge. It's a consequence of our power and intelligence and sheer ubiquity. The biologist and essayist Lewis Thomas put it succinctly, if depressingly: '… here we are, still nineteenth-century man, walking bootshod over the open face of nature, subjugating and civilising it. And we cannot stop this controlling, unless we vanish under the hill ourselves … We developed this way, we grew this way, we are this kind of species.' Dreams of empowering nature (which I often have myself) ring a little hollow in the light of this. The natural world plays no part in any decision to release it from oppression, which is always an act of largesse by us, reversible in an instant.

And being Earth's creatures ourselves, we too have a right to a niche. So in our garden we've had more modest ambitions, for 'parallel development' you might say, and a sense of neighbourliness with our fellow organisms. We try to embrace an inclusive idea of who 'the gardeners' might be, and imagine gardening *by* wild life as much as for it. We're also conscious of the world immediately beyond the garden. Our plot of land lies in Norfolk's flat, wood-starved arable plain, a region of intense chemical farming where not only many of the fields but the gestures at new hedging are wrapped in plastic. Throughout the twenty years we've lived here, the biological richness of the surrounding area has plummeted. Bird and insect populations have been ravaged. Road verges have become eutrophic from fertiliser run-off, allowing nitrogen-hungry plants to overwhelm more delicate species. We feel embattled at times, and that we should try to make some sort of small refuge, a natural oasis.

And an oasis in another sense too, because gardens have also been seen as retreats, places in which to play and feast and have a shot at the good life. We hope this has happened. The wilder parts of the garden have become a kind of outdoor resource centre, a Victorian walk with sudden intimate vistas, a den where children scale beech trees, cook primordial breads and carry out reverent burials of dead birds.

What follows is an account of my reflections on these issues and the occasional interventions they've prompted. It's organised roughly around the different habitats in the garden – the less governed, non-utilitarian areas for the most part, though Polly's inventiveness in adding a wild aspect to the vegetable garden is a heroic exception. But it's unashamedly discursive, in parts journal, memoir, treatise. It wanders off into other places and moments that have shaped my thinking and the subsequent writings that emerged. So the issues in this book aren't new. The difference here is addressing them in the intimate, pressing surrounds of a garden, which as the infirmities of old age advance, is often as much as I see of the world. When I walk round our patch, confident assertions and lyrical prose from my past have to face up to the hard realities of droughts and diseases and the ever-present barrenness of the farmland that surrounds us. I have arguments with myself and the opinions I've expressed. There are thwarted ambitions, philosophical musings, moments of delight and serendipitous accident.

This book began – and begins – in the climate-change-driven heatwave of July 2022, a new chapter of disruption hot on the heels of the pandemic. It was a moment when the world felt very precarious, and our small patch of it in jeopardy. The uncertainties and accidents proliferated, but some of them seemed to provide hope and meaning without any shaping by us. Those eventful days were an opportunity for reflecting on the ambiguous experience of inhabiting – and writing about – a garden in the midst of an environmental emergency.

2

HEATSHOCK

Sometimes it feels as if the climate crisis has become a grim competition. Temperature records are broken daily across the globe. Villages on our precarious Norfolk coast compare the number of houses they've lost to the sea. Acres of heathland incinerated by wildfires are logged on a rising annual scale. This month, July 2022, the daytime temperature has become match of the day. What began as an ordinary heatwave is turning into a 'weather emergency'. The forecasters are predicting the hottest day in the UK 'since records began', and amid the sense of general foreboding there's just a hint of civic hope at the prospect of topping the charts. On 19 July the record-breaking moment arrives. The temperature passes 40 degrees C at Kew and only a degree or so less here in eastern England. Out in the arable land beyond our garden, field fires are erupting, ignited by fragments of glass and the sparks from harvester blades. We watch our thatch nervously.

Outside, the heat feels material, some kind of thick fluid. I walk about in slow motion, feeling my senses dulling. Sounds are muffled. All delicacies of scent beyond parched grass and dust have evaporated. The fierce light on my ageing corneas is dotting the meadow with shimmering flowers unknown to science. Inside the house the small windows and thick clay walls create little nooks of cool where I sprawl in a daze. When I was young, everyone believed that opening all the house's orifices conjured up cool breezes, from who knows where. Now, scientific wisdom teaches the opposite, and we seal the house as best we can. But at midnight, claustrophobia overcomes me and I open the back door to let in what I hope is night-cooled air.

Something else wafts in with it. Pulsing out of the patio hollyhocks is an insistent rhythmic scratching. It's like radio static, or the rasping of dried-out twigs against each other. I think the heat must have gone to my head, and for a moment I wonder if it's some kind of electrical phenomenon of the charged air. But it's something more physical: a dark bush cricket. We've met them in the house occasionally, once clasped to a magnet inside the sewing box, but not often heard them singing. My insect field-guide describes its song as 'a staccato psst psst psst', which rather cleverly catches its air of whispered confidentiality. Unlike grasshoppers, which chirp by rubbing their hind legs against their wings, crickets stridulate by rubbing their wings together over their backs, a determined posture for singing out.

After the relentless heat, the cricket's riff feels like a benediction, a hint that not every shred of vitality has been burnt away. And that thought brings with it another whisper, a sliver of guilt. What does a cricket's song weigh against a creeping climate disaster? Should I resist being distracted by the tiny triumphs of the insect world, and stay focused on the gathering calamity? This is no ordinary heatwave. All northern Europe is enduring record temperatures and uncontrollable fires. Here in Norfolk, a large tract of Wild Ken Hill, the nature reserve used as a base by the BBC in *Springwatch*, has been turned to ash. We live further east, on the edge of Breckland, East Anglia's indigenous desert. The Brecks is a 400-square-mile sandbowl, an arena of frost hollows and strange mists and uncompromising aridity that amplifies every weather extreme. Today a field fire there jumped a garden fence and burned half a village street to the ground. In 1688, a sandstorm blew up in the bone-dry fields, a dozen miles south and buried the village of Santon, the place which four centuries later has just recorded Norfolk's highest ever temperature.

It's tempting to console oneself with memories of exceptional weather, which, back in the day, always seemed to pass, or at least be banished from memory. On this exact same date, 19 July, in 2006, eastern England was in the middle of another scorching heatwave. The temperature hit 36 degrees C and on a whim I decided to go on a hundred-mile expedition to my old haunts in the Chilterns, to search for the legendary ghost orchid. There was a touch of bravado in this (I remember willing the exterior thermometer on my old jeep to hit the 100 degree F mark) and a curiosity about what it might be like to be in a steamy beechwood, disorientated by its endless verticals and plagued by horseflies. But the wood was comfortingly cooler in the shade. I didn't find the ghost orchid, or very much else still growing on the parched woodland floor. I recall crawling about on all fours, trying to get a different perspective on anything that might be sprouting above ground level. The heat had not only put an end to any remaining flowers but had burned out all nuances in its internal landscape. The space seemed elemental: brown floor, grey uprights, deep green ceiling. The only sound I could hear was the crunch of my own footsteps in the dried-out leaf-litter. But on the way out I fancied that the trees arching over my head seemed less like the austere cathedral architecture they're often likened to, and resembled more the ribbed bottom of a boat, safely beached.

There it was again. The survivors (me included, I guess) in focus; the stresses an escapable backcloth. I have friends and colleagues who think it's inappropriate – maybe even unethical – to write in a celebratory mode in the middle of the climate crisis. It's fiddling while the world burns. Back in the 1980s I published a collection of journalism and miscellaneous writings, called *Landlocked*. There were pieces on the impact of the 1987 storm on Kew Gardens, on a winter break in the Camargue, on Don McCullin's haunting landscape photographs. One of its reviewers was the environmental editor of a national newspaper. His verdict was that, in the context of a world on the brink of collapse, my pieces were like 'postcards from Hiroshima'. His words stung, and seemed wilfully to ignore issues I had been writing about for decades. And, though the writer can't have known this, Hiroshima had imprinted my life from a very early age. I was a precocious four year old and avid TV watcher when the atom bomb was dropped on 6

August 1945. I was terrified by the newsreels, and became evangelical about the horrors of what had happened – which got me banned from our neighbour's house for frightening their daughter. I went on nagging people for the next few decades, and was gratified when nuclear weapons and environmental destruction began to be seen as linked forces in our disrespect for life.

What consoles me is that there *are* postcards from Hiroshima – of the gingko trees that remarkably survived just a few hundred metres from the epicentre of the explosion. Gingkos are ancient trees, native to the Far East, and have evolved through many climate shocks in their 200 million years on the planet. The heat flash from the bomb – global heating concentrated into a millisecond – incinerated their foliage and torched off the outer layers of bark. But the following spring the leaves returned and the trees flowered again. They continue to flourish and are venerated by the Japanese, who regard them as symbols both of the immeasurable destruction of that day and of nature's resilience. And, therefore, of hope. They call them *hibaku-jumoku* , the 'survivor trees'.

I think I see survivors – the gingkos, the arching beeches, the indomitable bush cricket – as biological anthems (from the Greek root *antiphon*, meaning response), songs of defiance against the forces of entropy. I don't believe that rejoicing in them implies complacency or denial. They are arousers, both in themselves and of our spirits.

I don't go on many expeditions to the wild woods these days. Entropy has become a personal affair, and the usual decrepitudes of old age have slowed me down and narrowed my horizons. Bad hips, muffled ears that won't pick up swifts' screams even with hearing aids, an arthritic spine that brings on spells of wearying stiffness. These are hardly existential problems, but they have changed my relationship with the natural world. I've become more physically passive – plant-like, you might say – hoping that things will come my way instead of energetically seeking them out. Witnessing rather than acting. During the pandemic I felt more locked in than locked down. But like almost everyone else, I shuffled about in a strictly limited territory, sharing what seemed like a universal experience of sharpened perception. We became aware of the taken-for-granted commotion of human restlessness. The quieting of traffic allowed birdsong to crescendo. The sky was clear of contrails. And some intimation of the fragility of human life made other lives seem more present, more precious. On my daily strolls round the garden perimeter – about a quarter of a mile, as much as I could manage on many days – new things jumped into attention. Distances seemed to concertina. For the first time I noticed that the viridian haze that surrounded our oak trees in early May was as much the fuzzy catkins as the young leaves. I admired a dunnock defying its anatomical ancestry and learning to cling to a hanging bird-feeder. In close-up I watched kidney-spot ladybirds stir from their winter retreats in fissures on the ash trees, and move about like slowly rolling balls of resin. My vision of the place had changed. The garden had become an amphitheatre in which I was witnessing old lives and new challenges facing up to each other.

Charles Darwin used to walk daily round his garden in Kent. He'd made a gravel track, which he nicknamed the Sandwalk (also, curiously, about four hundred yards long). He regarded it as his 'thinking path' and used it for pondering his emerging theories and for frolics with his young relations. There was a cairn on the route, and he kicked a stone away every time he solved a problem or spotted a pattern in his data. My perambulations are less rigorous. I wander round, stopping at stations for reflection, a long habit on favourite walks. In my young days in the Chilterns these pauses were at huggable trees, mysterious dells, sudden glimpses of something undefinable through a screen of tree trunks. Here in Norfolk they're more workaday: the patch where the wild daffs grow, a gap in the blackthorn hedge, a few square feet among the trees where the dog violets appear. I meander in a muddle of identities, as squire, witness, would-be conservationist, earthworm, trying to burrow out some modest niche for myself. And I'm repeatedly distracted by what I experience en route, and by the memories these stir up. I fret about what I've done in the garden and what I might do next, if anything. Did I leave enough long grass for cover and cocooning last time I had the meadow cut? Was it irresponsible to top up the dried-out pond with municipal water? The agricultural world glimpsed through the trees, with its ploughed and sprayed emptiness, jolts more global worries. South Norfolk is experiencing environmental crises way beyond the impact of climate change, as incompatible demands for housing, cheap food, energy and conservation converge on a finite area. The government has made a vague pledge to conserve 30 per cent of the land for nature. But things are going in the opposite direction. There are no new green spaces here, and every indicator of biological health is collapsing. We are all having to come to terms with the uncomfortable fact that the provision of sustainable energy and affordable housing are themselves the causes of damaging habitat loss and pollution.

A garden, with its complex interactions between humans and nature, is often seen as a metaphor for the wider world. But if so, is our plot a microcosm of this troubled arena or a refuge from it? I ponder these conundrums, until an idle spray of lady's bedstraw, first of the year, floats into my peripheral vision. Suddenly I'm filled with nostalgia for the chalk country where I spent much of my earlier life. Memories of walks and field trips, and the passages of writing and films that resulted, well up and are reviewed, not always favourably. Whole tribes of insects pass unnoticed while I debate with myself, and I'm reminded that what is going on here is always as much about writing as evolving a garden. After fifty years in the business I can't perceive the natural world without ordering it into shapes and sentences, despite knowing full well that much of it is inherently disordered and accidental. I'm a gardener with words in a way that I'm not with the actual life forms that share this plot. When the bush cricket sang in the crucible was I already primed, looking out for an anecdote, a smart heckle of the heat?

The bush crickets are singing in the daytime now, buried

somewhere deep in the sage and cistus. I'm reminded that this whole business of close literary attention to the natural world began with a cricket. On 20 May 1761, the Reverend Gilbert White interrupted his normally restrained and terse *Garden Kalendar* with an elaborate note on an event just beyond his garden in Selborne. With his brother Thomas he'd gone to 'examine the nature of those animals that make that cheerful shrill cry all the summer months in many parts of the south of England'. I'm biased when it comes to White. I spent the best part of a decade writing his biography and bringing his remarkable journals into print. I still marvel at his precocious vision of the natural world, and the prose he conjured up to describe it, and I find his account of the cricket unlike anything written about a lowly creature before.

The animal that had captivated White was a field cricket, *Gryllus campestris*, cousin of the dark bush cricket, *Pholidoptera griseoaptera*, now vanishingly rare in the UK. It has wing markings that have been described as resembling intricate wrought-iron work, and makes its chirruping by plucking the veins on its wings like a harp. In Selborne there was a colony on a rock-strewn and gorse-studded stretch of grass known as the Short Lythe. The brothers had gone out with a shovel, intending to (rather violently) dig the crickets out, but found 'in breaking up the ground, we inadvertently squeezed the poor insects to death'. And in a show of sympathy not at all typical of the time, they devised a more gentle extraction device: 'a pliant stalk of grass, gently insinuated into the caverns, will probe their windings to the bottom and quickly bring out the inhabitant; and thus the humane inquirer may gratify his curiosity without injuring the object of it.' Gilbert describes them with rapt attention, the male 'a black shining colour, with a golden stripe across its shoulder', its 'strong jaws, toothed like the shears of a lobster's claws'. He notes that near the mouths of their burrows, 'on a little platform which they make just by, they drop their dung; and never, in the day-time, seem to stir more than two or three inches from home'.

It is the affection mixed with this attentiveness that is so exceptional. The field cricket's shrilling 'marvellously delights' White, and he would 'be glad to have them increase on account of their pleasing summer sound'. A few years later (Gilbert was pioneering as a gardener as well as a naturalist) he 'endeavoured to transplant a colony to the terrace in my garden, by boring deep holes in the sloping turf. The new inhabitants stayed some time, and fed and sung; but wandered away by degrees, and were heard at a farther distance each morning; so that it appears that on this emergency they made use of their wings in attempting to return to the spot from which they were taken.' The draw of home, which is the central theme of White's writings, and especially of his *The Natural History of Selborne*, affected all manner of beings.

This poignant reflection exemplifies the tone of White's classic. He was no St Francis, but his writing marks a new turn in European attitudes to the nature. His attention to the living details of the world shades into a deep respect for it, and for the autonomous lives of its inhabitants. They are, if not quite his parishioners, at least his neighbours. And I like to think he regarded the creation of his would-be cricket sanctuary and the insects' construction of their little dunging platforms, their outside rooms, as analogous acts of gardening. Two centuries later, the field cricket's habitats had been all but wiped out by development and intensive framing. But, in an echo of White's far-sighted creation of an artificial home for them, the species is slowly returning to southern England, thanks to the kind of highly directed gardening we call nature conservation.

After a month or so, the heatwave settles into a sapping drought. The countryside has begun to look shabby, thrown under beige dust-covers. The grass verges are scorched. The birds look threadbare. Trees are shedding their leaves, three months early. Lines of scrawny hawthorn whips planted in the innocent hope that they might turn into hedges, have withered, broiled alive in their plastic cases. In the garden we sit and contemplate a scene of dissonant contrasts. The water in the pond has sunk so low that it's uncovered a forest of windthrown branches. I worry about what has happened to all the aquatic creatures that live there.

However there seems to be a thriving parallel universe. For several years, whenever we put our white garden furniture out for the summer, comma butterflies have joined us for tea. Now here they are again. The teatime troupes throng round us, doing threesome reels above the white table, settling on the white teapot and Polly's white hair. Their wings, scalloped triangles of marquetry, flex open and shut, then open wide again. They're sunbathing, and seem not to be visiting flowers at all, though there are plenty of drought-tolerant species (some appealingly white) still in bloom. On our few bits of lawn, where the grass has temporarily retreated underground, there are shoals of wild carrot, its lovely nested umbels looking like a crop of long-stemmed mushrooms. A neighbour's black cat wanders in among them, rolls on its back and begins swatting them as if they were toys dangled from the skies. For a moment the world seems blissfully, deceptively, held in poise.

The heatwave subtly changed our sense of home. We felt more vulnerable, less in charge of our own territory. We were aware that we had to adapt, and that there might be new opportunities as well as dangers. It took us back to the beginning of this garden and the hopes and visions we had twenty years before.

3

GROUNDS

The cow parsley was just beginning to go over when Polly and I moved into our new house: one moment in the subtle change between spring and summer. It was also not long after Rogation Day, listed in the liturgical calendar as a festival to bless the crops and relearn parish and field boundaries. And looking out over our unfamiliar acres, I was tickled by the fancy that we might Beat the Bounds. This was an ancient custom on this particular day. Parishioners processed round the fields, stopping at important trees and river crossings for readings of the gospel. The leaders carried willow switches to mark the spots, and if necessary add a little physical persuasion to the young people learning their place. The perambulation round Gilbert White's Selborne took three whole days. I felt we might do a more modest and secular version in the garden, to acknowledge what was there and make resolutions about the future. So we cut hazel wands from a bush in the hedge and set off, waving them at most objects in our path. The garden was slung between two arboreal poles. A large oak tree, about a 120 years old to judge from its girth, stood in the northern boundary. Its canopy was more than twenty-five metres across and I was impressed by the bell jar it created. To the south-east was a sizeable pond, dug we guessed to provide clay for the house walls, and the home of some busy moorhens. It was surrounded by yellow flags and dense bushes, and on the north bank an immense multi-stemmed ash tree erupted like a woody fountain. The base of the trunks suggested they'd once been cut at a level some way below the normal surface of the pond. They looked like mangroves in the still water. We pointed our wands towards them and I had a fantasy of floating little rafts on to the pond, planted up with sedges, like the floating reed islands on the Broads called 'hovers'.

Strung between and south of these two landmarks was a medley of trees and grass and cultivated beds, on which we quickly began delivering capital sentences. The dozen or so tall Leylandii would have to go. So would the hedge of dwarfed and jaundiced beech that surrounded the vegetables, and an island bed plumped with azaleas and hebes that would have been more appropriate in Cornwall.

Things moved very fast at the beginning. Within weeks the offending conifers had been cleared. At the same time we renamed the house with a more appropriate arboreal tag. The title given by the previous owners ('Cringle Cottage') was embarrassingly twee, and suited the stilted character of the garden design. We chose instead Mazzard, a vernacular term for the wild cherry trees that dotted our plot. It feels disrespectful now how casually we treated our predecessors' accoutrements, given we assumed without question that whatever we planned would last for ever.

★

A couple of months later I learned a little more about the history of the place. The farm (not named) figured in the 1836 Tithe Commutation survey, and was lived in by two bachelors. The accompanying map showed two rows of fruit trees in the front of the house and a pond at the back, exactly where it is now. Most of the rest of the back garden was part of an area labelled 'Hempland'. The pair were farming cannabis on what was now our back garden – the non-narcotic variety, used for making ropes and linen. South Norfolk was a centre of the hemp growing and weaving trade, much of it as a cooperatively organised cottage industry. Its high quality linen was sent to classy addresses, including the Russian Embassy and Eton College. Our neighbouring village had a royal warrant. This partly explained the survival of the pond, which was used in the processing of the hemp. The stalks were bundled and submerged in the water for a week, to be 'retted' so that the outer coating could be beaten free of the inner fibres.

We gazed over this melee and wondered what, in the long term, we wanted to do. Both of us wanted to loosen control, make a more equitable balance between the natural world and ourselves – grant a degree of self-determination to the plot and its inhabitants. And hope that the spirit of this philosophy might also permeate portions of the garden where vegetables or winter shrubs, say, were the important citizens. The idea of the garden as 'the outdoor room' was popular at the time, but the disciplines of exterior design, with its motifs and colour palettes and sightlines, didn't appeal to us. It seemed to bypass the fact that plants were living, often argumentative beings, with their own ambitions in life.

So being as realistic as we could, we decided to divide our responsibilities, though it it was hardly a fair apportionment. Polly, the energetic one, wise in the cultivation of things, would attend to the more organised parts of the garden, raising vegetables and making the best of the herbaceous border we'd inherited. I'd take on the wood and the pond and the rough grassland between. A soft touch, I admit, but philosophical pondering takes it out of you, too. I've always been foxed by vegetable gardening, bewildered by the refusal of these pampered plants to follow any botanical rules.

Polly set to work almost immediately in what became her very personalised style. She created strange-shaped beds, edged with stones or transplanted wildflowers – poppies, cornflowers, feverfew. She hung up switches of thyme as insect deterrents using bindweed as string. Soon a galaxy of other wildings made a bid to be the vegetables' ornaments: tutsan, thornapple (whose seeds must have been dormant in the soil), foxgloves and felt-leaved mulleins. It was about as wild and Wicca as it could be within the discipline of raising a crop.

Not long afterwards our builders, Roy and Lee, turned this vegetable corner into a walled garden. Because our house is a listed building, and this was within its 'curtilege', we had to use locally appropriate materials. So handmade bricks from a Suffolk yard and limestone mortar were trundled in. Before work started, we followed an old local good-luck custom and buried some of our hair in a bottle under the foundations. I loved watching Roy and Lee at their craft, laying bricks in Flemish bond, one pair along, one single across. It was as hypnotic as gazing at the tide coming in, and I had pangs of envy, wishing I could write with that easy rhythm. During the process they resorted to what I suspect was a piece of magic too – leaving a thin gap in the walls 'for the frost to flow out'. Meanwhile I reflected on the possible futures of the Wild End, whether to look forward, or look back, or both. I hoped Polly and I could both stick by the principles we'd committed to with our hazel wands, and she graciously agreed to accept a kind of tithe in the vegetable garden, 20 per cent to the wild creatures that scrumped and scavenged there. But there was one issue that would always separate our respective plots: fertility. The cultivated world thrives by energy being turbo-charged into selected crops; the wild by spreading nutrients among as many species as possible, a redistributive model of resource use. The compost would have to stay within bounds.

Gardens are often likened to theatres, with the gardener as writer, director and set designer rolled into one. But can't they also be open stages, frameworks in which natural forces – uninvited organisms, echoes from the past, vital processes of succession and decay – are welcomed to improvise their own landscapes? Maybe this isn't permissible within the strict definition of a garden. But all manner of ground plans and philosophies have been embraced over the centuries. There are cropping gardens, conceptual gardens, rose gardens, indoor gardens,

gardens with no plants at all. Japanese and Italian gardens celebrate pattern, while the English landscape garden pretended to a kind of studied nonchalance. I have a sneaking admiration for the grand confections of the polymathic seventeenth-century diarist John Evelyn. He was a lover of plants but also of human inventiveness. He wrote a vegetarian cookbook, a treatise against air pollution in London (in 1661!), and less happily, the famous tract *Sylva*, that helped form the practice of growing trees like arable crops. His garden at Sayes Court on the River Thames was full of jokes, scientific conceits and wonderful plants. He shaded his favourites with miniature parasols and created a hygroscope made out of water-sensitive wild oat seeds. The whole plot embodied a belief that what went wrong in Eden could be put right in the border. 'It is the common Terme and the pit from whence we were dug,' he wrote. 'We all came out of this parsley bed.'

At the other extreme there are virtual plots not even owned or worked by the 'gardener'; patches of countryside that are seen as personal retreats by those who know them intimately. The common feature of all these estates and refuges and parsley beds is that they are possessed spaces – not always in the sense of literal ownership or actual 'gardening', but from the net of meaning and purpose that someone has thrown over them. Making a decision to allow serendipity and natural processes as drivers fits comfortably into this definition. Of course they are also the possessed spaces and territories of other organisms, which are happy to accept the invitation to create their own pleasure grounds.

An early broadside against the presumptions of intense gardening was Andrew Marvell's poem 'The Mower Against Gardens', written while he was a tutor at Appleton Hall in Yorkshire in 1688. There are bigger themes lying behind the surface details: 'The Mower' himself represents an earlier pastoral world of simple, direct experience – mowing perhaps a more fundamental relationship with the natural world than sowing. Marvell lambasts enclosure, over-bred plants, grafting, and has a precocious insight into the ambivalent character of fertility.

> *And from the fields the flowers and plants allure,*
> *Where Nature was most plain and pure.*
> *He first enclosed within the garden's square*
> *A dead and standing pool of air,*
> *And a more luscious earth for them did knead,*
> *Which stupefied them while it fed.*

Jon Cook has pointed out to me the weirdness of the idea of enclosing air, and the ambiguity of that word 'standing'. Does Marvell simply mean stagnant, thus repeating himself? Or is he suggesting that the air is both 'dead' and somehow still alive? Zombified? I think he is conjuring the idea of a cell, an imprisoned space.

Two centuries later the idea that vegetal autonomy might not be incompatible with gardening was set out more explicitly. In 1881 the Victorian garden designer William Robinson published a book with the seemingly contradictory title of *The Wild Garden*, and subtitled 'The Naturalisation and Natural Grouping of Hardy Exotic

Plants with a Chapter on the Garden of British Wild Flowers'. His better-known classic *The English Flower Garden*, came out thirteen years later, and both titles share a hostility towards the regimentation of living things, be it in formalities of the Victorian garden, or the rigours of the increasingly organised countryside beyond.

Robinson learned his trade on an estate in Northern Ireland, where the dominant vegetation was carpet bedding. Tender and often garish plants were raised in greenhouses, planted out in straight lines and symmetrical formations (with exact spaces between each plant, left bare for contrast), allowed their brief season of brilliance and then dug out again. It was as if, as Robinson put it, they were carrying 'the dead lines of the building into the garden'.

He hated his time at Ballykilcavan, and left when he was only twenty-two, under rumours of an early act of eco-terrorism: marching out of the greenhouses, leaving the windows open, the fires out and carnage in the beds. He began to travel widely, visiting wild places and progressive gardens, and developing his guiding philosophy that gardens were places for celebrating the vitality of plants, and the ways that, given a chance, they would naturally mingle and spread in impromptu mosaics. His language of description was fastidious and original. He loved the sense of 'rightness' of plants allowed their natural settings: the unprompted hedginess of a wild rose scrambling over a fence, the glow of lemon globe-flowers in a dark, damp hollow; the way that flower and shrub and fern 'relieved' each other. He was captivated by a fernery in an artificial ravine in Yorkshire: 'To myself, coming from a region where monotony holds an almost unprecedented sway, where "decided" colours take too decided a lead, the relief offered by this exquisite touch of nature, of the sudden collapse of pot, bench and regulation, could only be equalled by a sudden transfer from a Bedfordshire Cucumber field to a Gentian-covered Alp.' Visiting John Veitch's famous nursery in Chelsea he admired 'the mystery and *indefiniteness* [my italics] which constitute beauty of vegetation in its highest sense'.

Robinson wasn't strictly an ecologist, nor a propagandist for vegetable rights. He never argued for complete laissez-faire in the garden. The wildness he loved was an aesthetic quality, and he was happy to intervene with subtle planting and ideas copied from the wild. But where is the line between aesthetics and ethics? Does a dissolving boundary between two plant colonies, say, suggest some sort of vegetal freedom as well as a satisfying design motif? Robinson also wrote that 'the true garden differs from all other arts in this, that it gives us the living things themselves and not merely representations of them', a step perhaps towards recognising plants' agency.

Robinson's use of descriptions like 'wild' and 'natural' would be contested in some quarters today. His mission, after all, was just a different regime for the growing of cultivated plants, many of them heavily manipulated and originating far from the home patch. A century and a half on, the idea of what is 'natural' is even more confused. I confess a certain weariness comes over me whenever I'm lectured on the virtues of 'reconnecting with nature'.

I've never entirely understood this, given that it would be impossible for us to live *dis*-connected from nature. The oxygen we take in with each breath is exhaled from the Earth's green vegetation. Our digestive systems contain self-organising communities of bacteria, which regulate even our mental health. We are cousins, at roughly calculable (if huge) degrees of removal, to every organism that has ever lived.

But I can hear my old philosophy tutor, John Simopolous, reprimanding me. 'Richard, you know very well what people mean when they say "reconnecting with nature".' Oxford philosophy in the 1960s had a strong interest in 'ordinary language use'. John once set me an essay on 'is a broken promise a lie?', and he would have urged me to respect this usage as signifying a *conscious* engagement with the natural world, and more ordinarily of a time spent outdoors with forms and systems of life that aren't entirely determined by humans.

Yet such a casual attitude towards the language we use to describe our relations with the rest of creation is now counterproductive. It's creating gross generalisations, false chains of cause and effect and dangerous hierarchies of organisms. The 'tree' trumps all other plants; 'pests' include any organism that someone, somewhere finds irritating. As for 'nature', I've collected a few of the more extreme uses of the idea over the years. Pride of place must go to the Tree Council's declaration during the great storm of 1987 that 'Trees are at great danger from nature' – thus placing the republic of trees entirely within the kingdom of man. During the Covid pandemic Boris

Johnson, in a rare moment of wisdom, remarked that 'we must be humble in the face of nature' – thus including the virus as part of the natural order, against the common view that it was an alien force. A year or so later, after devastating natural disasters in Greece, Pakistan and elsewhere, various presidents announced that 'we are at war with nature'. Volcanic eruptions, summer breezes, kitchen mould, tigers, pots of geraniums and cocktails made from herbs steeped in liquid nitrogen and touted as a remedy for our 'detachment from nature' – all are designated members of this ubiquitous pot-pourri. It seems that nature has come to mean 'anything that it not us' or made or caused by us. Bill McKibben's seminal book *The End of Nature* (1988) argues that our idea of nature as 'the other', a universe different from and unsullied by our human one, has been destroyed by wholesale environmental destruction and climate change, whose tendrils now reach to the top of Everest and the depths of the Antarctic ice sheet. Nothing is now immune from malign pressures that are *our fault*: the subtleties of spring weather, the migration of cuckoos, the summer evening moth storm – all things that we could once look to as independent registers of the world's proper turning. But now, just to complicate matters, we aspire to be included in this throng, not just reconnected but recognising, belatedly, that we are *part* of nature ourselves. Re-connection is redundant; it is implicit in the human condition.

The cultural historian Raymond Williams called nature 'perhaps the most complex word in the language'. Its original meaning was the essence or character of something.

Then it became a collective term for the material world, or some parts of it. The meanings extended and overlapped, and have been repeatedly given a moralistic spin to justify almost any ethical or political opinion. Nature as hostile, innocent, divine. The state of nature, nature red in tooth and claw, the natural order. Pestilence and birds of paradise. Williams talks of 'this reduction of a multiplicity to a singularity'. It's hard to know where to turn here. When a word becomes so inclusive, so all-embracing, it loses meaning. I often think we would do well to abandon it in all its abstractions and contradictions, and talk instead about the actual organisms and processes that comprise it. And we are hamstrung in modern usage by the very structure of our grammar, orientated as it is around subject–object relationships. A pertinent verb here is 'to grow'. Gardeners use it as a transitive verb: we cause growth. For plants it is intransitive, active: they simply grow. Between these two meanings, and the two seats of power they represent, we shuffle back and forth, trying to find our role in the world, and still regarding it as ridiculous to use the pronoun 'we' for anything beyond our own species.

4

QUILT

The house ceased to be a farm in the early twentieth century, and respectable turf was laid over the cannabis field. Grass gave way to grass. The hemp would have been more interesting, but times, and the law, move on. It left us with the challenge of what to do with the stretch of rough grass and trees that comprised the northern half of the garden. It had the look of a patch of municipal parkland. Simply continuing the previous owners' regime of regular mowing was not only deeply unattractive, but out of keeping with how we hoped our small estate would evolve. Action, or deliberate inaction, meant translating our vague and compromised ideals of naturalism and self-determination into specifics.

The conservation of existing habitats is based on straightforward ethical principles. We should give priority to all ecologically rich systems, especially those that have been evolving for thousands of years, and whose recreation is impossible with our current knowledge. But how do you begin to think about conservation when there is virtually nothing there to start with? 'Restoration' is the idea in which the strands of this process are usually twined together, and is driven for most people by a simple yearning: to enjoy some of the natural richness they remember from their pasts, back before Britain became one of the most nature-depleted countries on the planet. But the term restoration also suggests something more precise, the recreation of a natural state of affairs that existed at some particular earlier time. Which particular moment is not often specified.

A very long time has passed since the area now occupied by our garden was in even a halfway naturalistic state. It may well have been under continuous cultivation for three or four thousand years, bar a few spells as woodland during plague epidemics. So it's hard to form a picture of what you might aim to restore, between the poles of a mythic primeval forest and the 'traditional' landscape that preceded industrial agriculture.

There are various styles of response to this conundrum. One is to do absolutely nothing, and make the accidental principle all-embracing. Let the ground make its own decisions. Become a patch of scrub or a weed sanctuary. Grow into some spontaneous site-specific installation. If this proved to be a patch of waist-high docks and nettles, so what? This is 'nature' too. Yet I knew from the seedling oaks and cherries edging into the sward, exactly what that abandonment would eventually lead to here: a dense deciduous thicket, probably in less than ten years. Which would be a perfectly proper destiny, and convenient for us when we were too old to wield the strimmers. But not so much for the diverse habitat we hoped to encourage.

Another is at the opposite pole. Contrive a landscape

that's engineered especially for wildlife, with artificial ponds and boxes for nesting insects and birds, and plenty of planted flowers, especially those contemporary favourites, pollinator-friendly blooms. One option that's been touted on gardening programmes and extolled as a haven for butterflies and bees is 'the flowery mead'. This medieval conceit was a feature on the estates of the rich, and consisted of rectangles of short grass enclosed by walls or fences and planted up with pinks, primulas, lilies and the like. Giovanni Boccaccio's fourteenth-century *Decameron* describes 'a lawn of very fine grass, so green it seemed almost black, coloured with perhaps a thousand kind of flowers shut in with very green citrus and orange trees' – *Mille fleurs,* as one of their other names suggested. They were pleasure grounds, for strolling, making music, indulging in courtly flirtations. But they had a symbolic role as varieties of the *hortus conclusus,* visions of heavenly perfection on earth. In their current revival, they also have attendant angels: those revered *pollinators.* Other insects, busying themselves in ways that have no obvious benefit to humans, are often regarded as irrelevant, and occasionally as creatures of the underworld. I've seen some of these modern meads with their mixtures of poppies and geraniums and verbenas. They're very ornamental, and undeniable pleasure grounds for butterflies. But to me they seem less like restored wild spaces than herbaceous borders translocated into the surrounding lawns. A more promising variant of this approach is to be guided by the history and identity of the place, and attempt to take it back to some unspecified but more biodiverse state.

Reintroduce native plants that might have grown here previously. Bring back ancient management processes. The problems here are partly the guesswork involved in imagining this supposedly arcadian state, and the degree of goal-driven planning involved, which puts a rein on the freedom of its wild citizens, present and potential.

What hovers around these choices is the quest for that nebulous quality *authenticity*, which involves paying respect not only to the *genius loci*, but also its provenance, how it got to be. In the 1940s, the philosopher Walter Benjamin addressed an analogous question. His seminal essay 'The Work of Art in the Age of Mechanical Reproduction' discussed the impact of photography on the authority and charisma of original artworks. 'Even the most perfect reproduction', he wrote, 'is lacking in one element: its presence in time and space, its unique existence in the place where it happens to be ...' This includes the changes it may have suffered in physical condition over the years. What is lost by mechanical reproduction is what he describes as 'the aura of the work of art'. Reproduction 'detaches the reproduced object from the domain of tradition'. Benjamin wasn't over-impressed by 'aura', which he saw as appealing only to the privileged viewer. As a Marxist he was more interested in the democratising possibilities of reproduction, of making art available to ordinary people. An 'original' grassland or forest isn't an artwork or any other kind of human creation. But it has a provenance and 'a unique existence in the place where it happens to be' that isn't shared by off-the-peg butterfly gardens and organised plantations. The embedding of time, and the changes it generates, is a critical feature of natural habitats. The fashionable principle of 'mitigation' in which, say, a handful of planted saplings are offered as a replacement for a felled 200-year-old oak, ignores this.

Time is folded into natural communities by way of natural *processes*, and these don't get much attention if you're fixated on restoring a particular set of organisms or an exact moment in landscape history. Yet these processes – regeneration, colonisation, succession, connection, patination – need to be enabled and protected along with the organisms themselves. They are a natural community's way of life.

It occurred to me that commonland might be a model for a compromise between these possible futures. Lowland commons tend to be loose mixes of grass, scrub and occasional trees. They have ancient provenance and exceptional wildlife as a consequence. Yet they're habitats for humans too, acting in modest roles as goose-keepers, graziers, fruit-foragers, stick-gatherers and general encouragers of process. South Norfolk was once full of commons. When I looked at eighteenth-century maps of our patch, something like 30 per cent of the whole area was commonland. There were reed and sedge swamps (cut for thatch) by the River Waveney, and grassy pastures and meadows on the drier ground, used as rough grazing for cattle and geese. It was this usage that kept the sites open. But in the mid-nineteenth century, Parliamentary Enclosure set up shop and the credos of profit and uniformity replaced the virtues of natural and social diversity.

Many commons became exclusively private land and went under the plough.

We were lucky. Half a dozen commons survive within a couple of miles of the house. They're a diverse collection. An area of Lammas Land, cut for hay in early August (Lammas Day is 1 August) and abounding with cowslips and green-veined orchids in May. A small fen next to a row of what were hemp weavers' cottages. A town green awarded a warrant for a fair in the fourteenth century, heavily used but still with coastal species and a lovely and distinctively local pink-flowered yarrow. The Ling, an expanse of sandy soil supporting big patches of gorse and rabbit-grazed sward, with heather, sheep's sorrel, meadow saxifrage. And a few hundred yards down the lane from our house there is Brewers Green, whose turbulent history vividly tells the story of the tensions that accompanied enclosure.

In the 1890s the lord of the manor of Roydon was making tentative enclosure incursions around the parish. He impounded the geese and ponies of a few locals who didn't strictly have commoners' rights. He planted more than a hundred trees on the green, an imposition that historically had been a frequent prelude to enclosure (first trees, then connecting fences), and was widely viewed as an infringement of grazing rights. Unease grew in the village, and between August and early September 1893, a campaign of direct action was mounted by the commoners against the landlord and his agent, culminating in what's known as the Roydon Riots. It began when the impounded animals were set free by a boisterous crowd in Diss. Then the trees planted on the green were trashed and uprooted. The culmination occurred on the evening of a local election on 9 September, when a gang of commoners and hangers-on gathered in the pub next to the polling station and brewed up a plan for revenge against the landlord's agent. The meeting was lively, and in the words of the police 'there was a room full of men shouting, holloaing and drinking'. At 10 pm a now very agitated crowd, bearing an effigy of the agent, took off for his house at The Friary. There were broken windows and a running battle with the police that went on until midnight. Our house happens to be almost opposite The Friary and there is a story that it was used as a treatment centre for the injured. Subsequently the ringleaders of the assault were given comparatively short sentences. The lord of the manor did not press any other charges, and Brewers Green escaped enclosure.

The episode has a special meaning for me beyond that odd geographical coincidence. Twenty-seven years before the Roydon Riots there was similar direct action against an illegal enclosure in the parish where I grew up. The Battle of Berkhamsted Common in 1866 was set in motion by a local landowner and commoner with liberal leanings called Augustus Smith. He hired a gang of navvies to act as eco-mercenaries and take down the illicit fences around a large area of the ancient manorial waste. The commoners won the subsequent legal wranglings, and the affair kicked off a process that, via similar uprisings in Epping Forest and elsewhere, led to the historic Commons Act of 1876, the first piece of legislation to promote the preservation of commons rather than their destruction.

When we arrived in the parish the unenclosed green was managed by travellers' ponies, tethered so that they hard-grazed a circular area before being moved on to another patch. This was good for the flowers but not always for the hapless ponies, and they were eventually turfed off by the council. The green is now cut once a year, and has settled down into a pleasant sward of buttercups, knapweed and vetches.

One common that didn't survive the long tyranny of enclosure lay on the other side of our boundary hedge, and may have shared our pond. Encouraging a patch of rough grassland next door seemed the best reparation we could make. But how exactly to set about this posed its own problems, both practical and philosophical. One recipe for converting a lawn or a cultivated patch into a naturalistic grassland is drastic. You strip away the top few inches of topsoil, with its legacy of cultivation and that enemy of all wild ecosystems – fertility. Then scatter commercially bought wild grass seed and plant out pot-grown plugs of your desired wildings in artfully casual patterns, just as they did in flowery mead days. The reduction of two thousand years of nitrogen enrichment was the bonus of this approach, but I wasn't sure I had the stomach for such severe management. I also wanted to see what the subterranean seed bank might throw up if left to its own devices. Might dormant sorrels and ancient saxifrages be biding their time in the soil? Could the featherweight seeds of orchids have blown in on the wind? But one intervention was unavoidable if open grassland was the goal. There had to be some agency for keeping the wildwood at bay. We didn't think we were up to keeping stock on such a small area, so we would be obliged to stand in for the animals, become proxy herbivores. We would, periodically, have to put the existing vegetation cover to the blade. Cutting, the primal act of human control, loomed before us like the agricultural toil that was Adam's punishment after the Fall.

The first time we cut the grass we cadged the help of a farmer from the next village. He came in with a haymaker so big I quaked at the thought of it negotiating a way past the house. But he completed the mow in half a dozen swipes without a single bump against the fruit trees. We were left with half an acre of cut hay drying in the July sun, and the task of carting it about a hundred metres to a flat-bed trailer parked on the front lawn. We'd struck a deal with another local farmer, to swap our hay (for his sheep) for a several loads of manure (for our vegetable garden). It took us four days, on and off, two spent raking, turning and stacking, two more ferrying the dried hay in a tiny trailer behind a ride-on mower.

They were baking days, and in the southerly breeze the hay was as hypnotic as the sea, a shape-shifting, colour-changing surf, a spindrift of yellow rattle and clover bobs. It blew into our eyes and we saw the days through a haze of chaff. It crackled and soughed. It scented our clothes as if they'd been freshly laundered. At the foot of our amateur haycocks the seeds had already started to germinate (haysprouts, possibly the next culinary fad).

And it was alive. The cut had unsettled one set of citizens (temporarily I hoped) and tempted in another opportunist throng to eat them. The meadow teemed with spiders, mites, ants, centipedes and beetles, followed promptly by voles, frogs and juvenile green woodpeckers, whose scaly, barely feathered necks and long ant-seeking tongues gave them the look of predatory lizards. I rode about with a parasitic ichneumon wasp hitching a lift on my bare arm. It lays its eggs inside promisingly plump caterpillars, and I wondered what it saw in me. Above the garden, a sickle-winged hobby cruised among the swifts against the purest of skies, all of them munching our higher-flying refugees.

Talk about haydays. Were we playing peasant, enacting roles in the pastoral scene our garden adventure was always teetering towards? There was no economic need for us to do haymaking the old way, except to save us a few pounds on manure. (Though only a few. We got the bad side of the deal with a load of dung containing bits of dead pheasant and the remains of a burnt barn.) In later years we cut the meadow with a strimmer, and left the hay to dry where it fell. Then we advertised it as pick-up-your-own fodder for guinea pigs and rabbits. Small children swarmed about the grass with sacks and carrier bags.

Then we waited. The following spring it was clear that plenty of grassland species were already there, either as seed or vegetative plants. A few clumps of cowslips appeared, then a scatter of ox-eye daisies, and in high summer, knapweed and wild carrot. I intervened a little, in my earthworm mode. I scattered handfuls of seed – some gathered from local commons, some commercial mixes – wherever there was bare earth. There was no shortage of this: molehills, scalpings by the haycutter blade, deer root-lings. I did a bit of scalping myself with a rake, and once, fancying a bit of hunter-gatherer authenticity, set fire to a few square metres. And I planted three gorse bushes, to muddle the grassiness and provide a bit of cover, and because gorse is the totemic species of commonland.

And gradually, year by year, new plants moved in and the great annual procession began. First to come, while the grass was still short and mottled by winter moss, were the low-growing species: sweet violet (both purple and white forms), dandelion, celandine; cowslips, ground-ivy, cow parsley, buttercups, sorrel, the vivid blue pools of german-der speedwell followed. Then the great white oversheet of ox-eye daisies, with its understorey of clovers and birdsfoot trefoil leavened by the feathery plumes of sweet vernal grass, the most pleasantly named of all wild grasses. By July, the riotous technicolour mix of what ecologists call 'tall herb vegetation' – musk mallow, knapweed, agrimony and scabious, sometimes up to waist height – had settled in. It was like a constantly changing and evolving quilt, in which the boundaries of each patch flexed and shifted, but without ever seeming to overwhelm its neighbour.

Every so often a new species would join the neighbour-hood community. I was chuffed when sticky mouse-ear – 'sepals glandular with long white hairs extending beyond tips' – joined its common cousin (and chuffed that I even-tually identified it). Star of Bethlehem arrived in about the fourth year. Its blazing white stars only open in warm sunshine, and are deliciously teasing, lying low, half hidden by the grass, shining sixpences in a green cake. It may be native on local sandy soils, but here I think it leapfrogged in from the herbaceous bed. Yet the bee orchids by the path near the washing line were undoubtedly native and appeared as if by spontaneous generation, The nearest colony I knew was over half a mile away, but their seed is prolific and dust-like and could easily reach our garden on an easterly breeze. They lasted a couple of years and then vanished, only for their distinctive leaf rosettes to re-appear in a spot about five metres away. An easy journey for the seed, so I hoped they were the progeny of the original colony, although they can take two years to flower after the first leaves appear. We marked the spot with a pebble, and nudged competing greenery to the side every time we passed.

Here I must make a diversion to present the nudger: my walking stick. It's the device I use to negotiate with the garden vegetation. It was made for me by Rick Rickord, porter at Emmanuel College, Cambridge, where I was privileged to spend a spell as a visiting fellow – much of it under the meditative shade of the Great Plane (a kind of arboreal fellow) that adorns the college garden. It was the most generous and beautiful of gifts. Rick had crafted it out of straight hazel wand, topped with spalted yew and ringed with brass. He described it as a swagger stick, and there are gleeful moments when I chance my footing and whirl it about.

Sticks have always been connectors, fetchers and

pokers, reducers of distance, arguably the natural world's first tool. They've enabled all manner of beings to shape and interact with their environments. Twining plants seize on them for support, sometimes lifting them into the air. Woodpeckers and crows use them to winkle out grubs from crevices in trunks. Puffins have been witnessed picking them up in their beaks in order to scratch their backs. There's a Norfolk folk myth that woodcocks migrating across the North Sea carry a stick in their claws as a lifebuoy in case they have to put down in the water.

My stick is an elegant prop when I'm walking, or standing *contrapposto* to take the weight off my hip. But it's also evolved into a prosthesis, and a kind of wand. It brings closer things that I can no longer easily reach. I point at passing birds, swipe upstart ground elder, turn over leaves to see what's underneath, push stray seeds into the ground, move a little foliage to give a primrose flower a glimpse of the sun – or me a glimpse of a primrose. It's my Instrument of Minimum Intervention. I dream of a super-stick, with miniature secateurs at the end, and a yard-long microscope in the shaft.

And so, in those teasing days of March when the light seems to be touched with pollen, I use my stick to part the quilt and see what's coming up. It's a test of my eyesight and knowledge of vegetative growth, but also a slightly impatient scan for promises, as these diminutive sprouts navigate their way towards the spring. I can't always tell what they are. They're only centimetres across and a long way from my eyes. But I can make out trefoils of red clover, feathery sprays of yarrow, blades of ribwort plantain, thin needles of wild daffodils in their dedicated patch. As for the cowslips, their flat grey-green rosettes are everywhere, but as I lift their leaves I can see unidentifiable shoots lurking at the edges of the shade they cast. Everything is striving towards its share of the light, finding minuscule gaps between the larger leaves, making small diversions into the horizontal when free passage lies that way.

What I gaze for most expectantly, because they are small and distinctive and have such implicit power, are the seedlings of yellow (or hay) rattle. They stand out because of the symmetry of their leaves, held in alternate layers at right angles to each other. When they're fully grown they're topped with snapdragon-like flowers. The seeds mature inside large purses which rattle when they're dry, hence the plant's English name. But rattle's main activity is underground. It's what known in botanical jargon as a hemiparasite. It manufactures its own chlorophyll but takes sugars from other plants. My friend the ecologist Chris Gibson has peered into the extent of this parasitism, disentangling the underground connections between the roots of the rattle and other grassland denizens. He found that an individual rattle could be linked with up to seven other plants of several different species. Overall they can connect with more than forty different genera, many of them grasses. The effect of this is to sap the growth of the parasitised individuals, and give other plants more competitive chances. Yellow rattle is a subterranean herbivore. It grazes the meadow from below. It was one of the species whose seed I deliberately introduced in the hope that it would keep in check the rank grasses that were the legacy of the lawn. This it did, to a degree, but a good deal more too. In its fifth year the meadow began to turn tatty. A motley band of more substantial herbivores – pheasants, rabbits, muntjac deer – crept out of the cover of our trees and began nibbling flowers and flower buds as if they were cocktail snacks on stalks. They especially adored cowslips and buttercups, and I wondered if yellow had a special meaning for them. I wrestled for a while with the possibility of putting chicken wire round the most floriferous patches, but felt that a degree of chewing and fraying was essential in any habitat. It was evidence of a functioning food chain.

The meadow's general fraying was down to the hay rattle, too. Its population exploded, and for a while it became probably the commonest species in the sward. Which was fine, except that, as well as the grasses, it appeared to be leeching the pea family – clovers, vetches, birdsfoot trefoil. They were visibly shrinking. But rattle is an annual and by late July it had started to die off. Many of the parasitised plants regained their stature, and the areas where it had been densest became bare earth. The next spring these patches were colonised by a new generation of plants. There were no new species, but the distribution of the residents had shifted. This happens every year now, so that the components of the quilt are constantly shuffled. In some years the residue of its long farming history overcomes the rattle's grip and the grass grows six feet tall by midsummer; in other years we have bald patches.

I'm struck by the notion that whatever I might be doing to 'manage' the meadow, it's overshadowed by what the residents are doing for themselves. Birds crapping seeds. Insects browsing, pollinating, ferrying plant material. Parasites reorganising the vegetation. Marvell would have been delighted. In one of his couplets on the meadows at Appleton House he writes 'But Nature here hath been so free / As if she said "Leave this to me"'.

If you knew every interaction, could you see how they were related, predict the community's future? I suspect the grassland system behaves more like a crowd, a gathering driven by constant readjustment and shuffling and multiple feedback loops. And I'm aware that much of its life is happening underground and out of sight. Many of its plants are linked up with fungal partners via their root systems, their hair roots and the fungal mycelium physically sheathed together in a mutually beneficial network called a mycorrhiza. The plant shares the sugars it produces from photosynthesis; the fungus reciprocates with minerals and nutrients it gathers by breaking down organic matter in the soil. Our bee orchids are utterly dependent on this partnership. In older grasslands it seems as if the mycorrhiza may link plants of different species, and share nutrients and information among them just as in forests. Perhaps we could slightly modify the term that's become popular for these networks, and dub it the sward-wide-web.

Circumnavigating the whole garden in late April, I'm amazed by the spread of primula species inside these webs. Primroses have now reached our road verge and the lip of the pond. They line just about every path and have hopped over the wall into the vegetable garden. Some are the lovely pink variety, variously known as the 'churchyard primrose' or 'rhubarb and custard'. Botanists argue about whether this is a naturally occurring variety or a cross involving garden polyanthuses, but I'm not sure it matters. Here, on the corner of a shrubbery, it has double-crossed with a perfectly natural primrose–cowslip hybrid (known as the false oxlip) to produce a child's posy, a sprawling bunch of magenta flowers on top of a six-inch stem.

As for the cowslips, they've spread prolifically across the meadow and are colonising new niches even in the furthest corners of the garden. In May, it looks as if lemon curd has been spread across the grass. This is not how their expansion is described in textbooks, where they're categorised as 'clumpers', their heavy seed falling close to the mother plant, forming slowly expanding clusters and rarely reaching new areas. I guess their spread here has something to do with us, carrying their seeds about on muddy shoes and scattering them during hay cutting. But it also corresponds with the remorseless swelling of our red ant colonies. Some of their hills now come up as far as my knee. Ants have a symbiotic relationship with the seeds of primulas (and many other species). Attached to the seeds is a tiny globule of fat, called an elaiosome. The ants gather the seeds and take them back to their nests, where they detach the fat-rich parcel and feed it to their grubs. The seed itself is ferried to one of the ants' refuse dumps, where the organic matter gives it a good chance of germinating. (I've noticed that our anthills form a rough circle, like green standing stones. The area inside the circle is the only patch of meadow quite devoid of cowslips, and I've wondered if it's the ants' litter-free zone. I lament the fact that I'm not the kind of person who could establish whether this is fact or fancy.)

This symbiotic relationship between ant and flower seed occurs across the globe, involving many species of ant and thousands of different plant genera. It's one of the most remarkable examples of convergent evolution in which, over hundreds of millions of years, multiple species have independently arrived at the same mutually beneficial arrangement.

I've put cowslips seeds under my microscope, but am not sure I can make out the elaiosomes beyond a kind of slight waxiness at one end. I imagine what it would be like to witness an ant carrying a cowslip seed in its jaws, and envy the scientists who discovered this exquisite relationship. I picture them by their experimental hills, partially opened up, and watching the drama through their binocular eyepieces.

I've had an immersive experience with insect–plant symbiosis just once, and it changed me. I wanted to try and take a pollinating insect's view of a fly-orchid, one of my familiars. The glint of its blue waistband shining through the grass in the Chiltern scrublands is one of my hallowed botanising memories. Fly orchids are pollinated by a wasp species in an act which is called, with only the slightest of scientific sniggers, pseudocopulation. The orchid flower, like many in the *Ophrys* family, bears a slight resemblance to a wasp-like insect, with a brown oval body and petals standing in for wings. The male insect mistakes the flower for a female, and humps it. There's a vivid description of this erotic ritual by one of its earliest observers, the great orchidophile Colonel Godfery, in the 1930s. 'It alights on the lip, head uppermost, and rests there with quivering wings and waving antennae, doubtless a preliminary phase of courtship.' During this display, the insect's head is close to the orchid's sexual parts (real not pseudo), and with luck picks up a few pollinia, which it will transfer to the next flower it visits. I'd never been convinced that this is the whole story. It seemed improbable that an insect could make the visual error of mistaking a flower for one of its own, and suspected that other sensory cues were involved.

For once I decided to put regret and self-doubt aside and try to behave like a proper scientist. I'd make an expedition into the fly orchid's architecture. I couldn't responsibly gather flowers in Norfolk, where they're very rare, so I persuaded a friend to send me a couple of blooms from Provence, where the orchid is common enough to allow a little guilt-free picking. Several days in the post had dulled them, but I cut the freshest blooms and indulged in a spot of pseudo-foreplay. I sniffed them, licked them, and rubbed them against my lip. I couldn't register any scent at all, but the flower's body felt distinctly velvety, or more accurately like the pimply surface of a tongue.

I'm not sure what I was doing here, trying to simulate a wasp's sensorium. I sensed I was coming close to being a pseudo-copulator myself, and in danger of drifting into some anthropomorphic delusions. So I put the blooms under the microscope. At ten times I could make out a covering of fine hairs, emerging from a surface that looked papular and spongy. Might an alighting wasp *feel* it was clasping another furry creature? At a hundred times the blooms transformed into spangled landscapes. I could see the individual hairs, tipped with iridescence, as if they carried tiny globes of dew. Then I spotted two glowing crescents at either edge. They were made up of individual spots of blue, glowing as if they were LED lights. They looked like the eyes of an extraterrestrial insect in a computer game, and I remembered how important the colour blue is in insects' visual range. A few minutes later an extraordinary musky, meaty aroma began to rise from the flowers. I wondered if it was the volatile essence which the orchid produces to mimic the female wasp's sexual pheromone, beefed up by warmth from the microscope's lamp – the scent which presumably draws the male wasp to the flower in the first place.

This journey into the orchid's multi-sensorial interior was a transformative experience. It recalled for me the intense feelings of awe – verging at times on a queasy sense of unreality – I'd had about the material world as a teenager. I'd avoided formal biology at school, repulsed by the prospect of dissecting frogs and by the stench of dogfish in formaldehyde which lingered round the labs. But I had a deep sense of scientific curiosity (and a makeshift lab of my own at one end of my dad's greenhouse) and I wonder how I would have reacted if I'd made that journey into orchid inner space back then. I'm sure I'd glimpsed nothing new, but a long buried childhood longing to be a 'discoverer' had surfaced. I might have gone Darwin's way, set up an experiment on the edge of the beechwoods, manicured the orchids, created artificial ones on stalks with and without fur, and seen which the wasps preferred. Or would I have opted for the perspective I chose for the rest of my life: observed the intimate details as accurately as I could, then created an imaginative construction round them, a coherent narrative, an orchid whodunnit, regardless of whether the reality might be counter-intuitive and undramatic. I always hope these stories can be true both to the material universe and the imaginative engagement that is our species' special ecological gift, but I'm less confident than I was.

By high summer the meadow growth is up to my waist. I can't walk through it without creating a trail of bent stems. Even the moorhens are leaving little beaten tracks. In patches the vegetation is knitted together by another of the quilt's space-sharing devices: twining. Meadow vetchling and tufted vetch loop their tendrils round the stems of knapweed and the taller grasses, pulling themselves into vacant cylinders of air and light. I'm elated by the fact that the meadow is now a four-dimensional system, with its different citizens utilising not just leaf size and shape to negotiate living space, but direction of growth and time of maturation.

It abounds with insects enjoying this complexity: grasshoppers in the shorter grass, sap-sucking shield bugs on stems and leaves, hoverflies and red-winged cardinal beetles on the hogweed umbels. It's not all good news.

Some of the smaller butterfly species, such as common blue and small copper, are declining, although on one warm July morning I do a rough census of the meadow browns working the sward, count the number in a scatter of metre-square patches and then scale it up. I reckon we have nearly five hundred flying at once.

It's another excuse for putting off the annual cut. Andrew Marvell, up in Yorkshire, was distraught at the carnage haymaking caused among corncrakes. In his poem 'Upon Appleton House' he writes of 'the tawny mower' (still a heroic figure) recoiling from the suffering he is causing the birds: 'The edge all bloody from its breast / He draws, and does its stroke detest; Fearing the flesh untimely mowed / To him a fate as black forbode.' We don't have any ground nesting birds, but every year I'm troubled by the mortal consequences of the cut: the butterflies robbed of nectar, the squashed pupae, the trampled crickets, the abrupt vanishing of the tremulous carpet of colour. But in early August I do it anyway, for the sake of next year's growth. It's my *et in arcadia ego* moment. I leave stretches uncut for insect refuges: circles around the gorse bushes, and a strip at the border with the wood, where suckering blackthorn and seedling oaks are edging out and hinting at the emergence of scrub, something we badly need.

Back in the 1980s, I spent a while in Marvell's home county of Yorkshire in the company of some very different grasslands. I was making a film about limestone country (*White Rock, Black Water*), for the BBC's Natural History Unit. The Dales were where I'd first discovered the delights of limestone; its generous, mutable, accommodating character and exceptional flora. After decades of guilt worrying about why I was unmoved by the impassive granite of the Lake District, the supposed pinnacle of natural beauty and one of English poetry's motherlodes, I realised that I was simply on the wrong stuff. Rock-hopping on limestone in the Dales and the Burren in Ireland was a different kind of experience. It felt alive, mobile, made of much the same stuff as my bones. It wore out a pair of fashionable Kickers in under a week. In his poem 'In Praise of Limestone' W. H. Auden calls it the 'stone that responds'.

These limestone grasslands were relics of how vegetation began to return to the land after its scourings by the glaciers. And looking back, I think they taught me that 'grassland' – even in the garden – did not actually have to be grassy. It could be bumpy, rock-strewn, waterlogged, alternate between wood and open land. Grasslands lead inexorably to other kinds of habitat, unless they're kept open by extreme weather or grazing animals. Or by us.

Our spell in the Dales was spread over three months, and I commuted from the Chilterns in what proved to be a summer of cold wet weather. In some ways this was a blessing, pumping up the river flows and forcing waterspouts from the cliffs. But we were glad to spend a night indoors, filming inside Ingleborough Cave where the limestone, leached out of the surface rock by rain, re-deposits itself in fantastic gargoyles of tufa, like calcareous sponges. We tramped up to a boneyard of frost-shattered boulders on Moughton Fell and recorded a brass band concert in the natural amphitheatre by Hardraw Force waterfall.

But much of the time we spent on grasslands that were quite unlike those in the south of England. Rocky river floodplains, steep pastures dotted with mountain pansies, and limestone pavements where polished tables of rock, scraped clear by glaciers and cracked by earth movements, are eaten away along these fault-lines by rainwater. The deep cracks are called grykes and the flat tables clints. Plants grow in both situations, wherever small pockets of soil have built up, and the whole panoply resembles an elaborate rock garden.

But the topography posed real problems for exploring, let alone filming. Some of the grykes were a metre wide and up to two metres deep, demanding nervous leaping rather than a leisurely stroll. The absence of standout surface features was disorientating and meant it was hard to re-find rock formations and plants we had scouted out and thought filmworthy. At first (into the accidental even then) I fancied presenting this sequence as a piece of unrehearsed *cinéma vérité* leaping from clint to plant, and hoping that a sense of spontaneous discovery – 'Look at this!' – might make its own point about the capricious diversity of the place. The director and the cameraman quite rightly scotched this idea as an impractical ego trip. In the end we resorted to marking up about an acre of pavement with a grid of ribbon-decked bamboo poles and waymarkers. It looked as if we were laying the ground plan for a garden-with-rooms, or a route map for pollinators. We also had sent up from Bristol a contraption for lowering a film camera into the deepest grykes, to capture a plants-eye view of these microhabitats. We dubbed it

The Arm, though it was more like a inverted periscope. It arrived without its balance weight, and miracles of make-do were achieved with two rucksacks and a pile of limestone pebbles.

Thirty years on I'm looking through a folder of snapshots I took while we were filming. They're little cameos which, without my really having this in mind, illustrate ecological and human ingenuity intertwining. Here is the camera's first descent into a gryke, a monstrous Gothic cloister grooved and fluted on both sides, and ever so slightly moist. Here is Caroline, our director, posed behind a spontaneously arranged bouquet of ferns in a bowl in the rock – which in turn may have been formed over thousands of years by a pebble grinding away in a surface pool. What made it a posy – history or our aesthetic sense? And there is the cameraman Richard, four feet *below* the surface, his shoulders wedged between the walls of the gryke, filming wild garlic that had been drawn up more than metre towards the light. The grykes, generous with humidity and dappled shade, are full of woodland plants: early purple orchid, herb paris, solitary primroses and rivulets of bluebell. There are trees and shrubs too, mostly driven down into subterranean existence by wind and grazing animals. One ash tree, maybe centuries old, had adopted an entirely horizontal existence, winding along the lip of a gryke and sprouting here and there into bonsaid domes. On the damper clints there were clumps of species found in northern grasslands and meadows: bloody and wood cranesbill, pools of butter-yellow globe flowers, tufts of bird's-eye primrose, whose coral-pink flowers and glaucous leaves looked as if they had been alchemised from the very stuff of the rocks. And at the point where the flat pavement began to slope down on to the hill, a drift of lilies of the valley. Their broad leaves clattered in the wind, which carried their divine scent to us as we crouched over the grykes, not quite sure if we were filming a rock-bound meadow or a dwarfed wood.

5

ARK

Woods always beckon you in. I walk the path into our patch of treeland most days in spring (always anti-clockwise – a habit since childhood) and love the sense it gives that we have the custody of a proper wood. I pass a bank of washday-white stitchwort – 'shirt buttons' in Norfolk – and turn north into the trees. Ahead is a stretch of track that appears to vanish enticingly into a grove of multi-stemmed ash trees. It's lined with primroses and moschatel and a small patch of wild garlic. Sprays of new leaves hang over the path, layers of different greens catching flecks of sunlight and moments of shade: hornbeam, field maple, the felted foliage of whitebeam. I brush the leaves with my hand as I pass. They're moist, gel-like, newly hatched. The cherry blossom is already going over and its windblown petals form chaplets around the trunks. I remember these cherry garlands encircling whole woods back in the Chilterns.

It's a vision of an English wood in April – except that for the most part it's an illusion, or at least a contrivance. I planted the wild garlic and the maple. The track which seemingly disappears into the depths is no more than thirty metres long, and has to turn a sharp left when it comes up against the ancient hedgebank that marks our northern boundary with the bleak farmland beyond. I say to visitors 'come up and see our bit of wood'. But it's tongue in cheek, and I'm embarrassed to flatter the plot as 'woodland'. This will sound like pedantry again, and I need to explain why I think it's more than that. Woods aren't just collections of trees. They have origins, histories, evolving structures, internal landscapes, unique identities. And in a way that mirrors this, so do our perceptions of them, which can be scholarly, devoted, scientific, romantic. I've experienced all these modes, sometimes simultaneously.

What was up at the far end of the garden when we first moved in was a stretch of grass studded with a collection of broadleaf trees about three or four decades old, chiefly ash, cherry, beech, horse chestnut and whitebeam. The grass between them had been regularly mown, so there was little leaf litter and no seedling trees. It was a small plantation, an artefact. A lot has happened in the twenty years since, and moments of real woodiness have begun to occur. A couple of trees have come down in gales and the ground is strewn with dead brushwood. Bramble and blackthorn have spread, plus a whole new generation of seedling trees. As for the flowers – there's primrose, early dog violet, dog's mercury, herb bennet – I think they moved in from the old bank and ditch that edges two sides of the tree patch, and which may have been the boundary of the common. I doubt that many other woodland plants could migrate in naturally, so bereft of real woods is this corner of Norfolk. In the Middle Ages there was a large tract of forest half a mile away called the Heywood, and at some indeterminate time before that, the postglacial mix of woodland and open ground. It would be nice to think they had left some echo. I try to imagine seeds biding time in the soil, waiting for the trees to return, but a few thousand years is a long stretch. Should I be planting these lost or absent species – bluebells, wood anemones, goldilocks – to speed up the development of a richer woodland ecosystem? Or see what develops of its own accord?

What I did was influenced by feelings and ideas about woods that had been evolving, often in contrary ways, since my childhood.

What makes a group of trees a wood, in our sense of place? Is it simply a matter of age and size? A subtlety in the play of light and shadow? An inkling of some deep stability, or of processes of ancient succession? When I was a boy, the woods I knew seemed like caves, places of retreat and mystery (and danger: aged eleven I was seen off at gunpoint by a keeper). I wriggled into the hearts of hollies, hung out in the latticed branchwork of cedars and hugged beech trees – not out of some spiritual longing, but because I relished their solid, maybe erotic physicality. I loved above all the sense they gave that nobody knew where I was. I think this was part of my dim early understanding of what 'wild' meant.

A few years later I found my primal forest, the place where I first learned the hierarchies of woods and their entanglements with human affairs. It lay about a mile north of the Field, a ribbon of trees that climbed south from the valley of a chalk stream, the inelegantly named Bourne Gutter, which was regarded locally as a Woewater, and believed to flow only in times of great trouble. But for my romantic teenage soul it flowed with the quicksilver of the future and the faraway. On my bike ride to the school games field I'd stand on a high point and gaze at the glittering ribbon as it lost itself in the woods. The view made me feel slightly strange, and the back of my legs tighten as if I was gazing down from a great height. I can't explain this, except that part of it was a kind of nostalgia foretold, an instinctive sense that I would hold and long for this view for the rest of my life.

I didn't get inside the wood for years. It was heavily fenced and belonged to a notoriously aggressive farmer. But from a footpath along the eastern boundary I began to get a handle on its rough contours. There was a larch plantation at its foot, created by Italian POWs in the Second World War, which blended into what may have been an ancient hazel coppice. Then an area of chalk scrub, which at the crest of the hill morphed into a mysterious clump of tall beeches. A while later, when I got into more serious historical investigations, I found a large-scale eighteenth-century map of the wood and saw that the beeches – just a dark smudge on the horizon from my teenage viewpoint – was called Heathen Grove. What did this mean? Had it been an outpost of the notoriously pagan Hellfire Club further south in the Chilterns? The burial spot of some eminent local atheist? Its cryptic name egged on my courage as well as my curiosity and at long last I wriggled through the barbed wire.

In the years that followed I began to peel back the wood. Its aged sections lay below each other like rings of bark. The Lego wood, the planted grid of larches. Then, a little higher, the beginnings of naturally sprung woodland. I became attached to this section, and took picnics there on summer evenings to sit among the marjoram and listen to the Proms on a portable radio. There was no path to Heathen Grove from here, and I had to shoulder and sometimes crawl my way through the mesh of sprawling hazels and wild roses. But the orchids! Spotted, fly, white helleborine, broad-leaved helleborine, twayblade, the species of scrub and woodland growing close together. As I got closer to Heathen Grove itself, the scrub thinned out and more mature trees began: holly, field maple, beech. But they were not as majestic as they looked from a distance. Their size and scatter suggested that they'd sprung up about a century ago. In no way were they some heathen equivalent of the 'green cathedral' to which mature beechwoods are often likened. But the ground beneath was like the Elysian Fields, carpets of bluebell studded with early purple orchid. On the barer patches were dog violets and the true oxlips that my fellow plant hunter Jamie Robertson and I had recently discovered in a group of local woods, a hundred miles from their presumed exclusive locations in East Anglia. And threading through them all were ribbons of something scarce and beautiful – coralroot bittercress, a species which only grows in a few gravelly woods in north Bucks and some patches of the Kentish Weald. It's a plant of extraordinary grace, like a woodland lady's smock, with large pink flowers and purple-brown bulbils at the base of the leaves. This combination of ancient woodland species is unique. They grow together nowhere else in Britain, and had probably been on this site for thousands of years.

But it brought me no nearer solving the mystery of Heathen Grove's name, so I'll invent a story. In the medieval period it had been part of a much larger stretch of ancient woodland. Sometime in the early eighteenth century, when ancient British cults were fashionable among antiquarians, the owner cut out or interplanted a faux-sacred hilltop grove. This is when the site got its cryptic, possibly tongue-in-cheek tag. During the nineteenth century it was felled for its beech timber, and what is there now is the subsequent natural regrowth of both trees and ground flora. I like to think this is a plausible tale, and would describe a very satisfying multi-layered culture–nature sandwich.

But in my late thirties I wrote this in a book about the cultural history of Britain's wildflowers: 'Our ideal wood is green and snug, light and roomy, with a few secret glades and dark corners to add hint of romance, but not so big that we cannot find our way out.' It reads like an estate agent's puff. Had I really come to believe that this was the prescription for the nation's 'ideal' wood? Or mine? More decades on I can see what had happened. I'd been seduced by Louis MacNeice's poem 'Woods', about the Dorset copses he knew as a child, but had completely failed to understand its duality. It's a dense, reverberating poem. He talks of his father, who 'found the English landscape tame', and how as a child, Louis loved the copses' 'dark /But gentle ambush', the feel of 'caterpillar webs on the forehead ... And the mind adrift in a floating and rustling ark'. Yet 'grown six foot tall', and rather tree-like himself, he concedes his father may have been right. His Dorset woods weren't like'the wilds of Mayo, they are assured/ Of their place by men ... And always we walk out again. The patch / Of sky at the end of the path grows and discloses/ An ordered open air long ruled by dyke and fence'.

MacNeice lived in my stretch of the Chilterns towards the end of his life, and drank in a pub I used. His portrait hangs over the corner chair he occupied as an austere presiding bard. Out of the window he could see another kind of wood, the hanging beechwood that clings to the western edge of Chiltern scarp. It's one of the steepest slopes in the region, not quite the wilds of Mayo, but a long drift of self-sown, gale-prone trees, and home to lilies of the valley and elusive orchids. MacNeice's poem counterpoints these two types of woodland, the tamed copse and the wild forest, and they were the two archetypes that shaped my perception of woods in the years that followed.

But no woody place is ever just one or the other. The ancient copses I roamed like a prospector were cultural artefacts – 'assured of their place by men' – but always on the point of escaping into self-determination. They had vernacular names, precise medieval banks and centuries-old coppice stools, neatly re-cut every ten years or so. I gradually learned the keys to their authenticity as living monuments. They had irregular outlines, odd-shaped trees and suites of finicky plants ('ancient woodland indicators') that rarely colonised new plantations. I parsed these features like an antiques connoisseur, as if they were forest finials and tapestries. But between cuts – and between the trees – the woods went their own way. Older trees shed branches and grew smaller leaves to cope with drought. Seedling trees took root. New ground plants appeared, their seeds carried in on deers' feet and tractor tyres. The carefully engineered structure turned feral at its edges.

In their turn, the Mayo-like wildwoods aren't wall to wall trees. Nor are they lacking in cultural histories. Near the foot of the climb to Heathen Grove there's an unmanaged wooded common. One summer a group of travellers set up camp there and began cutting firewood. They stood on the roofs of their caravans and lopped the tops of the overhanging hawthorns with chain-saws. The results – trees with bushy regowth high up and known as 'giraffe pollards' – are still there, monuments to an unusual moment of sustainable harvest. And I've twice walked through the Axmouth–Lyme Regis Undercliff, the chaotic jungle created when a huge slab of chalk cliff collapsed on the Dorset coast in 1839. Mature beech trees came down with the cliff, many landing the right way up and taking root. Colonisation by thorn and hazel and ash quickly followed, and the whole spontaneous forest is now a dense tangle of old and emergent trees knotted together by lianas of ivy and old man's beard. It's one of the most accidentally created and unmanipulated woodlands in England. John Fowles, who used it as a key location in his novel *The French Lieutenant's Woman,* wrote later that

'It looks almost as the world might have been if man had not evolved.'

But what happened in December 1839 was not an uncomplicated natural cataclysm. This stretch of the south Dorset coast is naturally unstable, and when the first chalk floe slid away, it left a chasm into which the next layer collapsed. There was a wheatfield on it, already showing its young shoots. It fell intact, the right way up, like the beech trees. And the following August it was cere-monially reaped. Ten thousand spectators gathered for the harvest, with the reapers led by young women wearing brooches in the form of sickles. Was it a celebration or a wake? William Turner Dawson's watercolour of the event shows the wheatfield as a vast amphitheatre, sur-rounded by chalk crags. On top of one of these is a group of picnickers hoisting the Union Jack – southern England showing its stiff upper lip.

In the 1980s I bought a wood of my own in the Chil-terns, the full story of which I've told elsewhere. It too had a complex identity and history. A third of its sixteen acres lay under a hundred-year-old beech plantation. The remainder was the unkempt relics of an ancient wood that had been largely clear-felled in the Second World War. The natural regrowth was interplanted in the 1960s with hybrid poplars for the match trade. I bought it for mul-tiple reasons, partly in the hope of restoring it to some undefined earlier unblemished state, and partly, I think, to have a place where I could run wild among the trees as I had when I was a kid. I ran it as a community project with the local village, but it presented the same ideological challenge that I have with the garden. How could we strike a balance between allowing the wood some self-determination, encouraging its ecological renewal, and having a bit of forest fun ourselves?

Looking back, I think we did quite well. We never had anything as organised and domineering as a management plan, but talked a lot about what we felt about the place and what we might do. There was a general agreement that it needed more light, so the clearing of the matchwood poplars and a thinning of some of the dense inherited regrowth were priorities. Beyond that, everything happened pretty much free-form. Folk began to tread out a network of paths, following badger tracks and desire lines. Glades began to form where the local primary school held an Ascension Day service among the bluebells, and where their older siblings had parties and sleepovers after exams. The wood responded magnanimously to our potterings. The ground flora, which was already exceptional, began to move around into newly enlightened spots. Fussy plants like sweet woodruff and lady fern popped up in the beech plantation. Ash seedlings abounded. Holly trees massed into a grove. Buzzards returned to nest. Along a vehicle track we'd excavated to provide an exit route for timber, colonies of the exquisitely liquorice-striped, sweet-pea-scented wood vetch erupted, presumably from buried seed. It had been regarded as extinct in Hertfordshire for more than twenty years. The sweet irony was that much of this happened accidentally. It was a collateral blooming, cashing in on the small disturbances we'd caused.

I spent a lot of time by myself in the wood, just pootling and watching its intricate flora evolve. But I often took a pair of heavy-duty loppers with me, and clipped the brambles round my favourite primrose patches so that they would make a better show. I pruned low-slung cherry branches to makes arches over the tracks. I lopped sycamores that were shading ashes, and ashes that were shading young beeches, as if I had certain knowledge of the proper hierarchy of trees. The excuse I made to myself was that I was doing much the same as the local badgers and bark beetles, making a few corners of the wood commodious for myself. William Wordsworth once chided a landscaper for this kind of tinkering, warning that 'a man little by little becomes so delicate and fastidious with respect to forms in scenery: [that] where he has a power to exercise a control over them and if they do not exactly please him, in all mood, and every point of view, his power becomes his law.' But I reckoned I deserved a niche too. On reflection I think this is what all of us involved with the wood were after. Not some officious sense of dominion or stewardship, just the chance to feel a part of the place, and become, for brief moments, modest woodland creatures ourselves.

I learned many things from these woody excursions. That there is space inside the ecology of woodlands for us to be both human actors and wild accomplices, if we get the scale of our engagement right. That we can view naturalness as a process as much as a state. I thought of the ways in which I could apply these lessons in our small patch of treeland in Norfolk. I hoped that natural regeneration would eventually fill the empty spaces between the original plantings. But I did intervene, putting in a scatter of hornbeam, field maple, hazel and spindle saplings, because I was unsure whether these species would make it in by themselves (they did). I gave them no stakes or tree guards, did no watering or mulching. This was chiefly an ethical choice. I wanted them to grow as freely as possible, and build up their resistance to wind and drought as a bonus. I've never understood those who believe that trees can't prosper without human supervision, and how they imagine Britain became naturally forested before such intensive care strategies became fashionable.

The new trees prospered. Deer nibbled the young stems but not enough to bother them. Soon the planted saplings were joined by self-sown seedlings. Oaklings arrived on the edges of the tree patch, and wherever light penetrated or slid under the canopy. Cherries sprouted in the shade, from suckers as well as stones. Bird-sown hawthorn and blackthorn appeared, and hazel and hornbeam. Most gratifying was the clump of small-leaved, or East Anglian, elm, *Ulmus minor*. I think this began from a now dead elm on our boundary bank. Small-leaved elms spread by suckers, each suckering shoot a clone of its parent. The mother tree in the wood is now about fifteen years old, but still free of Dutch elm disease, and surrounded by an increasing number of its progeny. Normally the beetles which bore into the living bark and carry the fungus arrive in about the tenth year.

What I'm doing, or more exactly allowing to happen, couldn't really be described as re-wilding. The area is

minute compared to the landscape-scale projects now
under way all over Europe. We have no serious earth- and
tree-moving herbivores, and the ground hadn't been under
trees for quite possibly thousands of years. But the principle is the same: allowing natural processes the major role
in how the place evolves. So maybe 'wilding' without the
're-'. The woodland ecologist George Peterken has coined
the useful terms 'present naturalness' and 'future naturalness' for the processes and goals when human interference
is largely taken away. But I interfere a bit. I keep a path
open, lopping a few branches, and shifting windblown
brushwood with my walking wand. A case of stick on
stick. And I plant a few clumps of ramsons and moschatel,
wild specimens from a local friend's woody garden.

I'm not sure it has been enough. The countryside
around our garden is almost bare of old woods. a huge biodiversity deficit. I miss them badly. There are a couple about
five miles to the south, with scarce and wonderful flowers,
including a lungwort that grows nowhere else in the UK.
But they're dedicated to shooting pheasants and are heavily
keepered. The owner most generously allows the public in
on one day each year, coralled in a feudal cart towed by a
tractor. I'm not agile enough these days to brave the barbed
wire (or the keeper), but when I was, I found them tainted
places, the ground dotted with piles of rotting birds, and
with nettles from the eutrophic release pens and feeding
stations spreading over the early purple orchids.

There aren't many attempts to encourage new treeland
in our region. The most conspicuous new features are

in vitro hedges, long lines of plastic tubes with the occasional green sprays protruding. It's early days, but it may be centuries before these evolve into the classic English hedgerow, that meandering, bushy-bottomed thicket of blossom and blackberries, honeysuckle and rose, with singing warblers and gothic trees buried in the greenery. More than 150,000 miles of these linear woodlands were grubbed out by farmers between the end of the Second World War and the 1970s to make way for the big machines. I've no doubt these new plantings are being created with the best of intentions, to restore the lost miles and contribute to carbon capture. But I find it hard to understand why they're being done in just this way. The starting point are spindly whips, about eighteen inches tall, mostly of just one species, hawthorn. They're enclosed in plastic, either wrapped tightly round or in short opaque tubes which also contain a stake. The consequence is that most low growth is suppressed and the bushes resemble lollipops, smaller versions of what the great chronicler of landscape ecology and history Oliver Rackham once mocked as 'gateposts with leaves'. A few years on they are flailed every winter, drastically reducing their blossom and subsequent fruiting. The resulting hedge is a leggy artefact, a standard boundary unit about two foot wide by four foot deep, mulched by a detritus of plastic and of minimal value for wildlife. Some never get this far. The failure rate is high, a consequence of poor quality nursery-grown stock, careless planting, and constriction inside the tubes. In some of the large-scale plantings along trunk roads in East Anglia, more than

50 per cent – some hundreds of thousands of young trees – have died.

The origins of hedges are mired in myth and pseudo-history. Most of us were taught at school that they were invented during Parliamentary Enclosure and date back no more than a couple of centuries. But the first hedges were created in the Neolithic, as tribal boundary markers or stock-proof barriers. They often originated in strips of woodland retained during deforestation, bulked up or extended by 'dead hedges' of cut or fallen wood. The planting of saplings was a later development, and in the medieval period many hedges were grown from seed. One favoured method was to twist acorns, haws, sloes and holly berries in a rope of old cloth and bury it in a shallow trench – no need for any sort of guard as the thorny species protected the rest. New tree and shrub species arrived of their own accord, their seed blown in by the wind or excreted by perching birds. In the 1970s the ecologist Max Hooper developed 'Hooper's Law' which suggested that, as a rule of thumb, one new species arrived per thirty metre stretch every hundred years. So it was possible to give a rough date of origin to hedges. Back in the Chilterns I walked weekly along a meandering Saxon ridgeway lined by hedges with at least fifteen species per thirty metre stretch, a transporting journey through the pre-Conquest landscape.

The hedges round our Norfolk garden don't really follow any of these rules. Along the eastern flank there is a substantial bank-and-ditch, almost certainly the boundary between the farm and the one-time common. The bank in such situations was always on the near side of the ditch, to present grazing animals on the common with a formidable climb if they tried to pillage the cultivated acres. It's topped with what are now quite mature trees – field maple, oak, ash and, unusually, once-coppiced common lime trees. These are a riot of bees in flowering time, which transform them into one of the few trees you can hear a hundred yards away.

Along our western boundary is a much more modern hedge, planted I imagine when the next door house was built half a century ago. It was originally pure hawthorn, but it's already broken Hooper's Law and has three new colonising species: sycamore, cherry and holly, which gives me some hope for the ersatz hedges in the fields beyond. I'm especially pleased about the holly. This is now quite scarce in Norfolk hedges but used to be planted deliberately to provide sight markers for plough teams.

All these green barricades – including the straight quickthorn rows that were put in during enclosure – were highly functional. They were to keep stock contained and mark the boundaries between fields and properties. In East Anglia at least these purposes are now fading. Fields are being amalgamated into immense prairies and stock raising is declining. Wildlife conservation and landscape ornamentation are now probably the chief reasons for retaining or creating hedgerows, which means the new plantings need to be evaluated from that perspective. So why are so many planted with a single species in narrow lines? Why the tubular tree-guards that distort the natural form of the shrubs, and leave a quantity of plastic litter that would not be tolerated if it had been fly-tipped? The usual explanation is that young trees need protection from wind, frost and browsing animals, particularly rabbits (currently scarce in Norfolk). Deer, horses and sheep are more plausible threats, but they of course can reach what is growing out of the mouths of the tubes. A few land-owners (mostly cottagers) have taken the risk of planting hedges without security blankets, and the results are, miraculously, thriving.

The love of hedges has deep roots in our popular culture, our language, our folklore, in centuries of land-scape painting. These are good reasons to conserve existing hedges and create new ones, provided they are biologically rich and have a reasonable chance of maturing into wildlife corridors. But with the topography of the farming coun-tryside changing so fast, maybe it's time to experiment with new kinds of boundary features. Greatly widened ditches, for instance, could support shade-loving plants and, if wet enough, whole aquatic ecosystems. Leaving five metre uncropped strips around the edges of fields, a scheme recently introduced and financially supported by government, is promising. The strips are allowed to develop into rough grassland with just a portion being cut each year, but sadly aren't permitted to progress to scrub. Or we could follow Henry Thoreau's vision and bundle all those hedgelets into a single parish treeland: 'Every town', he wrote, 'should have a park, or rather a primitive forest of five hundred or a thousand acres, where a stick should never be cut for fuel, a common possession forever, for instruction and recreation. We have cow-commons and ministerial lots, but we want *men*-commons and lay lots, inalienable forever.' I'd be more tolerant of stick-cutting than Thoreau, but his vision is a warm one. A 500-acre plot is just one kilometre square, pretty much the area in our parish recently given over to maize grown for bio-fuel.

But I doubt Thoreau would have expected his 'primitive forest' to be planted. If it wasn't already there, it would have sprung of its own accord, by the simple removal of cultivation. I've long been intrigued by our single-minded dedication to planting trees, as if we have begun to doubt their biological ability to reproduce themselves. The most frequent question I was asked about my Chiltern wood was 'When was it planted?' as if it were inconceivable it could have grown spontaneously. I'm sure the tree-planting urge comes from a generous desire for reparation, to make good the damage we have done to the planet, to 'make the forest grow again'. Trees are immeasurably valuable organisms. They lock up carbon dioxide from the atmosphere, filter out pollution, refresh urban landscapes. In their maturity they provide habitats for all manner of living things from goshawks to algae. And the act of planting can be a vivid and direct way for people – children especially – to engage with their local environments and to grow a sense of responsibility for its protection.

Yet alongside this, wild trees establish themselves and prosper without any of the intensive care we feel obliged to give planted saplings. Trunk road verges bristle with blackthorn and wilding apple trees. Thickets of ash, oak and sycamore erupt along railway embankments, their leaf-fall sufficient to slow down trains. Conservation organisations spend much of their management energy clearing self-sown trees from their reserves: oak and hawthorn from downland, willow from fens, birch groves from heaths. All cases perhaps of trees in the wrong place. The condition of woodiness is irrepressible, what most lowland habitats will turn into if given the chance. In our garden I've counted eighteen species of self-sown trees since we moved here: cherries in the meadow, oaklings in the borders, hawthorn by the pond, a yew behind a shed (which we've used as a Christmas tree), dogwood (welcomed) and elder (not so much) in our Mediterranean bed. Over the past twenty years I've watched three small local paddocks being colonised in the same way and becoming what are now thickset young woods.

There are many sites where trees don't quickly establish themselves – parks, school grounds, and the bare acres of pig ranches and poultry farms, for example, and anywhere where regular maintenance suppresses them. (Equally there are trees planted where they're not ecologically desirable: round here that usually means on commons and damp meadowland). And in these places, planting is the best way of establishing new trees.

Yet when you look closely at the planting reflex, the rituals that surround and follow it, the way it is lauded as a panacea for all environmental ills, it's clear there is more going on than the heartfelt desire to sequester carbon and make reparation. These are the instructions for aftercare that went with a planting kit from the Tree Council: *'Tending.* Check the tree in March or April every year ... Fill in any gaps in the soil around the roots ... If the soil is waterlogged channel/drain excess water away from the tree ... *Pruning*. Careful pruning can prevent problems in later life ... If a tree has two competing upright shoots remove one at an early stage to leave a single main shoot ... *Clearing*. Pull up any grass and weeds for a radius of at least half a metre round the tree ... Early in the year, when the soil is moist, cover the cleared area with a mulch mat, bark or brushwood chippings or an old piece of carpet.' This, remember, is the care regime recommended for a wild, native organism, not a delicate house plant.

Does it matter how a community of trees arrives provided it settles in and thrives? Is there really any difference between a plantation and a naturally sprung wood? Plantations are usually very uniform. The trees are evenly spaced and evenly aged, and very little is able or permitted to grow under them. 'Natural' woods tend to be untidy, densely vegetated and bearing trees of all ages. The saplings that have sprung from acorns and fruits carried in and cached by birds and mice are in a place that plainly suits them, and within a few years begin to look like a young wildwood. What is telling is the way in which such naturally sprung trees are often bulldozed out to make way for planted ones. They're dismissed as 'scrub', seen not as a community of young trees and protective thorns, but as a shrub-level weed. The landscape architect Nan Fairbrother once described scrub as 'the state of original sin in our landscape'. It is as if the human hand on a young tree gives it some extra sanctity or blessing, and perhaps blesses us in return. There is something paternalistic in the process of embedding the sapling, the cosseting and watering, the privileging over competitors. The young tree is treated like a dependent child. Maybe this is a productive relationship, generating a sense of responsibility and what is often called 'stewardship', but it can shade all too easily into a belief that trees are intrinsically feeble and reliant on us for their very existence. This is part of that ancient arrogance – stretching back through the Doctrine of Improvement to Genesis's 'dominion over' – which put the planet into its long fulminating state of crisis.

Looking at our patch of treeland in Norfolk I'm aware that my sharp, ideological contrast between the planted and the naturally sprung is simplistic, and a piece of human-centred arrogance itself. 'Natural' growth and inventiveness begin the moment after planting. The trees that were put in half a century ago – luckily a tad haphazardly – are beginning to look magnificently shaggy, and have already formed a closed canopy. The trees I planted myself twenty years ago – more uniformly than I realised – are growing well, though with a rather dull uprightness. But I don't see them as 'my' trees and find I have no emotional attachment to them. Paradoxically it's the self-sprung upstarts that have earned that – the cranky oaklings and suckering cherries and ribbons of blackthorn now forming a ragged understorey. I admire their resilience, and am grateful to be a witness of their autonomous lives. I don't so much look after them as look out for them.

The one tree species that isn't regenerating well in our garden is ash. We have the five trees planted around the 1950s, a large coppiced individual in the hedge and the undateable giant by the pond, but only a few seedlings. Every spring I gaze nervously up at them, peering for signs of a premature and possibly terminal autumn as ash dieback edges across Norfolk. Mostly I worry about the pond ash. It's a spacious, elastic tree that defines the character of this corner of the garden. Its lower limbs are close to the surface of the pond, and in a good wind they ebb and swell like breakers on an incoming tide. Occasional branches snap off, and one has pitched into the water and stuck, its broken end protruding about a foot. It looks a perfect kingfisher perch, and we await a passing winter migrant on the lookout for a rest.

The whole tree is in an intimate relationship with the pond, but I'm not sure how it came to be there. Its three stems begin well below the current level of the surrounding ground, and look as if they were last cut back about sixty years ago. They may even be separate trees growing close together. The bottom few feet of the trunks are under water for six months of the year, and as the level falls over the summer, something like a miniature swamp is exposed. Birds bathe and feed at the edge. I've glimpsed a female redstart ferreting for grubs, and an upside down great spotted woodpecker hanging from the subterranean roots and sipping from the surface. Once a heron came down in a mist to stand vigil at the edge, unaware that there were no fish to catch. When the water level rises, mallards and their families sometimes visit. One winter a drake mandarin, in all its regency pomp, swanned up and down a few times and then took off through the ash branches like a guided missile.

But the ash pond's totemic species – and the whole garden's really – are the moorhens. They've been residents all the time we've been here, and have become our beloved familiars. We've dubbed them Methodists for their earnest demeanour and purposeful scuttling. They're always busy and vocal, but not often successful parents. They've nested in the yellow flags, in a tuft of purple loosestrife, in the dark and scrubby enclaves at the very back of the pond. Sometimes they build trial nests which are never occupied. The chicks – usually four to eight – are zigzagging about the water catching insects almost as soon as they've hatched. But the adults take them for not very well shepherded walks through the meadow, where they get lost, and are picked off by crows and stoats and once by an enraged mother mallard. In most years only one or two of the chicks make it to adulthood. It's enough, in the great scheme of things, but I grieve for their depletion and have forced myself think of them as mayflies, flashes of exuberant life enjoying their brief moments in the sun.

So far our ashes are disease free, touch wood. But I'm under no illusions about the future. Ash dieback first appeared in the wild just a dozen miles north of our garden in a village called, with what is now dark irony, Ashwellthorpe. Its parish wood has many dead trees, and a few isolated survivors. But no long thread of stricken ashes stretches down toward us. I've only been able to find a handful of dead trees within a two-mile radius of our house. Many more have symptoms (thin foliage in the canopy, some clusters of dead leaves) in summer, but appear to recover by the following spring.

There is still much that is unknown about the disease. It seems to be caused by an oriental fungus, or a mutant of a harmless European species, carried west and north by global heating and the commercial trade in saplings. It first appeared in eastern Europe in the 1990s, and showed up in the UK early in 2012 on saplings grown in continental nurseries. What is shocking about this is not just the slovenly practice of exporting British seed to the Netherlands to be germinated, then reimporting the saplings back to Britain; but that it was thought necessary to produce nursery-grown stock at all in a country where wild ash seedlings grow like grass in many places. The Ashwellthorpe outbreak seemed unconnected to the contagion in the tree nurseries, however, and was probably caused by spores carried on the wind from the continent.

Britain has about 200 million ash trees, and it is our third commonest native hardwood. I've seen the devastation dieback has already caused in some parts of the country, and even in the best-case scenarios the epidemic will cause dramatic changes in local landscapes and ecologies. Across Europe about 70 per cent of all ash trees are dying. But it is not doomsday for the ash. Some trees appear to have a degree of resistance to the disease, which may not be full immunity, but enough to reduce the fungal infection to an annual irritation, like black spot in sycamore. This is partly genetic and partly down to the existence – only recently discovered – of a protective microbiome of bacteria and fungi on ash tissue. Ashes are very variable genetically. We see this in our own trees, which have visibly different twig densities and leaf colouration and whose coming into leaf stretches over a spell of three weeks. What worries me is that this diversity doesn't seem to stretch to their gender. Ash trees are bi-sexual, or, more accurately, gender fluid. Their exquisite flowers – sheaves of purple filaments that resemble miniature sea anemones – can be male, female or hermaphrodite. Individual trees tend towards one or the other. But in any year, a branch, or an entire tree, can change sex. Only the females and hermaphrodites produce the winged seed. Alas, all our trees seem to be resolutely male, and I have never seen a single ash key on any of them. If there is a disease resistant tree among them, it will be the last of its line.

Back at the pond ash, the moorhens have tried a new nesting strategy. They've scaled one of the slanting stems and, just where it levels out, have built a nest in the ivy. It is six metres above the surface of the pond. The sight of the adult birds using their cumbersome feet to tree-climb was something to behold. The almost invisible nest was a success, and we were lucky enough to be there when two of the chicks belly flopped down into the water, celebrating the long communion between tree and pond. For them at least, it didn't matter if the ash was alive or dead.

The gale ripped through the garden one late summer night. It combed out twigs and leaves, splintered branches and left us the gift of a thicket, the one feature our patch of treeland lacked. The wind in East Anglia, you're invariably told on fetching up here, 'comes straight from the Urals'. Now, climate-change charged, it barrels in incessantly from the west. That night it broke off one of the lower branches of our big oak – a substantial piece of wood, a schooner's boom nearly fifteen metres long. It had snapped at its junction with the trunk, cantilevered down through about twenty degrees and felled a couple of dead elm bushes and a hazel in the boundary hedge. Plus a vast quantity of ivy and bramble. The result was a tangle of lianas and twiggery, the kind of arrangement that in Norfolk is called a 'muddle'.

The thing is, this wasn't some random anonymous branch. It was the serpentine limb I'd written a short biography of five years earlier, peering through binoculars at points where damage from wind and ice had forced slight changes in its life story: I'd tried imagining it as a three-dimensional graph, logging the branch's adjustment to overshading and wind exposure. For a few feet it became a whirlpool of wood. It bent to ride over the branch beneath, which in turn was trying to evade this intrusive sunshade. At the point where the two branches came closest together there were U-bends, bark erosion and sheaves of compensatory twigs. John Ruskin, in a passage in *Modern Painters*, gives a warm description of this internal negotiation in oak trees. 'Every branch has others to meet or cross, sharing with them in various advantage, what shade, or sun, or rain is to be had. Hence every leaf cluster presents the general aspect of a little family, entirely at unity among themselves, but obliged to get their living by various shifts, concessions and infringement of the family rules.' A minor family squabble is a tad anthropomorphic, but probably closer to the truth than the all out war that would doubtless be declared in a TV documentary.

Now the shifts and concessions had become rather

drastic. But I found the result exhilarating, dynamic, *hopeful*, and the new thicket became the focus of my daily perambulations. I wondered what might happen in it, emerge from it? A couple of years later young trees began to poke through the sheltering lattice of bramble and ivy: field maple, hawthorn, elm, hazel, sycamore, even a sweet chestnut. A grass snake burrowed into the leaf litter. The collapsed branch itself began to bristle with new vertical shoots. The climbers began to recede and the whole zone turned into a natural shrubbery within the wood. What had begun as a minor setback for the oak had turned into an opportunity for its neighbours.

What this oak never makes me feel is *calm*. Excited, nervous, intellectually intrigued, yes, but never purged of stress and worry as seems to be the popular therapeutic role assigned to trees. My friend James Canton has written a book about the state of transcendental calm that envelops him when he is under an 800-year-old oak in Suffolk. There is no arguing with the evidence that walking in woods – or any half-natural environment – has quantifiable benefits on a huge range of health indicators from mood to blood pressure, but not many suggestions about why this should be. I'm sceptical about the 'forest bathing' theory – that exposure to the volatile exhalations of leaves strengthens your immune system, cures cancer, lowers anxiety, etc. (An oak tree's vaporous messages are principally an early warning system about aphid attacks.) So how does it work? Is it the switch in attention to something outside the self and its nagging preoccupations? A deep memory of our own wild origins?

Yet the consequences of 'nature therapy' aren't wholly benign. Seeing nature as a commodity whose purpose is to make us feel better seems to me to diminish it. We're centre stage again. Mark Cocker has written 'I don't see much distinction between a message telling us how great nature is for our well-being and the biblical concept that man shall have dominion over everything upon Earth. Both converge on the idea that nature is instrumental to our purposes. It exists to meet our needs.' It would be hypocritical of me to go this far, because I 'use' nature to meet my need for hope. But what does bother me is the one-dimensional focus on achieving peacefulness. 'Calm' is an uncommon state in nature, which is full of busyness, experiment, peril and tragedy, even beyond our calamitous mistreatment of it. I have watched a swallow showing all the body language of grief over its mate, killed by flying into a plate glass window. I have grieved myself over one of our moorhen chicks, entangled to death in a burdock, and convinced that it was in some way my fault for tolerating the plant. Wouldn't a mature therapeutic engagement with the natural world take in and empathise with these realities of life in the wild, rather than sweeping them under a carpet of the pretty, the charming, the restful? The default affective state of almost all living beings is an intense attentiveness, not to the self but to the world beyond. It might not be a bad goal for us, too.

6

VISITORS

An unexpected consequence of the branch collapse was that I was able to see in close-up the leaves of our big oak, which had been obscure while they remained hidden in the high canopy – and, I confess, taken for granted. Now I gazed at their deep jagged lobes, the lack of little ear-like 'auricles' at their base, and realised with some embarrassment that what we had as the defining growth of our tree patch was not a 'heart of oak', the impeccably English *Quercus robur*, our immemorial national symbol, but a *Turkey* oak, *Quercus cerris,* an interloper hiding in plain sight. I sped round the garden and saw that a good number of the self-sown oak saplings were also this species. Was I inadvertently giving sanctuary to a land-hungry foreign invader?

Turkey oaks were introduced to this country in the mid-eighteenth century, probably from Austria. They're native in central Europe and the Middle East, grew in the land mass that was to become Britain 150,000 years ago, and probably would have returned here after the last glaciation if the English Channel hadn't opened. They're almost indistinguishable from English oaks at a distance and began to be popular plantings in parks and hedgerows. Their wood is prone to splitting, so they're not much use as timber. But they've proved to be more resistant to pollution and browsing than English oaks. They're also more successful at regenerating, perhaps because their acorns have more tannin, and are cached by jays and squirrels rather than being eaten fresh. Our tree was probably planted as a boundary feature at the height of their popularity in the Victorian era.

But there's a twist in this part of the story. In the 1950s, a gall wasp *Andricus quercuscalicis* arrived naturally in Britain. It was originally a native of the same area of Europe as the Turkey oak, and was maybe tracking its slow northward spread. It's an insect with a remarkable lifestyle in which two generations link the two species of oak. The first generation lays eggs in the catkins of the Turkey oak, provoking the formation of tiny conical galls around the larvae. When these hatch the wasps fly to English oaks and lay eggs in the young acorns. The chemical disruption caused by the second generation larvae distorts the acorn growth into something resembling an eccentric ecclesiastical headpiece, lumpy and warty and known as a knopper gall (from a German root meaning knob). Knoppered acorns aren't fertile, and in trees heavily affected, between 30 and 50 per cent of the acorns can be knocked out. Back in the 1960s, when the galls became widespread enough to be noticed, there was panic about a possible arboreal apocalypse. I remember headlines warning of the imminent extinction of our national tree, and even the Forestry Commission warning that knoppering could lead to the 'emasculation' of the English oak. No such thing has happened or is likely to happen. There are plenty of acorns left to replenish the population even after heavy gall-wasp occupations. What may happen though, because of the Turkey oak's slightly better reproductive potential, is that its seedlings will make up an increasing proportion of wild oak populations. This may not be an entirely negative development. Turkey oaks are hardy, resilient, successful, and host to a fair number of the insects and fungi that live on our native oak. They could be a small bulwark against the ravages of climate change.

There are other immigrant trees in the garden. One is the big cherry plum that canopies the south-west corner. It's a native of eastern Europe and central Asia which was probably introduced to Britain in the late medieval period, and then became naturalised. Nobody is quite sure, as it's been repeatedly confused with blackthorn (smug botanists call it 'fool's blackthorn'). But it's invariably the first blossom of the year, often out by early February (with smooth leaves appearing with flowers, if distinction from the sloe bush is puzzling). I've no idea whether our specimen was planted by a previous occupant, is a relic of an old hedgerow or arrived as a bird-sown wilding. Its froth of white flowers edges out over the lane and back across the climbing roses, and I can see it through the bedroom window when I wake in the morning. It's one of my anthems against the winter, but I love it too for the memories and associations it carries. It was a common hedgerow plant back in the Chilterns and a kind of clan marker. Pure cherry plum hedges were a signature feature of land belonging to the Rothschilds. The white lace it threw over the hedges in spring was followed in fruitful years by knots of small yellow and orange plums, known as 'myrobalans' or 'mirabelles'. Or, as a friend jokingly reconstrued them, 'merry-bellies'. They were sweet and sour and vivid and we made merry-jellies from them – and still use our Norfolk ones in cooking. Cherry plum's natural hybrids with blackthorn are believed to have played a part in the complicated evolution of the domestic plum.

I've a tally of more than a score of foreign visitors which have found their way into the garden and settled down. Most originate from southern Europe, and some regard the space as Liberty Hall. Evergreen alkanet haunts every corner, lining the paths, edging the walls, growing clean through some of the shrub roses. It's scratchy and stubbornly rooted but makes fetching posies with cow parsley in May, cobalt blue stars studding the white foam. Russian vine, dramatic in full tasselled flower, sprawls over one of the sheds. There is an expansive tansy by the oil tank, giving off the nostalgic scent of childhood chest rubs as you brush past. Sometimes mysterious plants appear just for a season. A small-flowered bugloss, an annual of fields and waste places in the Mediterranean, scrambled about in the gravel one summer. Its pleated blue flowers had short stamens, not protruding beyond the petals like the flickering tongues of its cousin viper's bugloss. Had its seeds arrived here stuck to our walking shoes after one of our tramps in Provence? When I wrote a book about so-called weeds back in 2010, I argued that intruders and freeloaders aren't always happenstance arrivals but often side-effects of our personal affections and behaviour. They're reflections of the work we do, the walks we take and the people we are, with our individual histories and hoardings.

The more familiar immigrants have pasts and attachments too. Mugwort and small nettle may be descendants of the weeds that grew in the hemp field two centuries ago. The chickweed and shepherd's purse in the lettuce belong to a lineage that may have been brought over in the seed corn of Neolithic farmers (themselves immigrants from southern Europe) who broke soil in south Norfolk three thousand years ago. We tend to think of weeds as invaders, I wrote, 'but in one sense they are part of the heritage of a place, an ancestral presence, a time-biding genetic bank over which our current buildings and tended gardens are an ephemeral shell'. I like the idea of foreign colonisers as archaeological artefacts, embodying history as if they were arrowheads or old manuscripts. But in another way they are nothing like museum specimens and are mischievously alive.

Plants move and settle, dig in and blow away. Their seeds slip out on the wind and stick to the moorhens' feet. Oregano has jumped from a herb bed into the meadow, and flourishes despite annual decapitation. Whole root systems hitch rides to the bonfire corner, including *Phlomis russelliana* from the Middle East, whose yellow-flowered flagpoles have established a little outpost there surrounded by native primroses and red campion. They are all plants 'out of place', or out of the places we have assigned for them.

*

At its most fundamental level a garden is about boundaries, both literal and metaphorical. Its limits are where your control, or your imagination, sets them. There are beds and fences, territorial and cultural claims, visions and memories. These boundaries, needless to say, are porous and contested. Organisms and definitions move across, in both directions. An aspirational tree becomes an emblem of a neighbour's light-hogging unneighbourliness. In a matter of inches a wildflower transforms into a weed. One summer during a spell of dogged west winds, the seed pods of our yellow rattle (a wildflower to us) were whisked up from the meadow and blown through a gap in the blackthorns into the next door field. The following year a plume of yellow (defiantly weedy to our neighbour) bloomed among the rye grass. But we've been punished for our unruliness. One edge of our garden abuts a minor road, and we're tolerant of the wild flowers that spread across the verge in steadily ascending waves, from primrose to hogweed. But the neighbours complained, and one weekend we returned from holiday to find that an anonymous vigilante had mown the whole lot flat. In the borderland itself, cultural mores and wild enterprise are in a ceaseless tussle.

We inherited one particular kind of boundary. The house itself is surrounded by a continuous strip of gravel, a substance often used to make what amounts to a stone moat, a clear transition zone between brick and earth. I think it's also seen as a cordon sanitaire, from which squatters and intruders can be easily hoicked. But the loose stones make the most seductive of seedbeds. Anything that floats past may alight and take unrestricted root. I've watched processions of parachuted seeds – hawksbeards, valerian, willowherbs – heading east on summer breezes, then dipping down by the shelter of the house and heading for this inland beach.

During the heatwave a curious growth took root here in the shade of a wooden table. It first appeared in the late spring, an undistinguished sprout with spear-shaped leaves which branched and crept about in a vaguely upward direction. Now it's come into bloom, with a mop of brilliant yellow petals. It was obviously from the daisy family, but not anything I could place as a native species. So I rummaged through Eric Clement's splendid *Illustrations of Alien Plants of the British Isles,* and there, between Ragweed and Rudbeckia was a clear image of our visitor: Niger, *Guizotia abyssinica,* native of Ethiopia, and cultivated for the oil from its seeds. It's acquired a modern use as wild bird food, and is the favourite snack of goldfinches (a strange pairing, but I suppose no more so than peanuts and blue tits). We have a feeder with Niger seeds, but it's a good twenty metres from where the plant sprang up, so I like to think the birds perch on the table, and crap on the gravel. I regard it as the goldfinches' vegetable garden.

There's an apocryphal story about a small girl who reads the label on a packet of bird seed and asks, with admirable logic, if birds grow from the seeds. No, mum replies, they eat them. The seeds are duly sown, and next morning the patch is covered with busy birds. *See,* says the child ...

The gravel is spangled with flowers at most times of the year, in serendipitous and often gorgeously unscripted combinations. Scarlet pimpernel creeps among the marigolds. Buckwheat sprouts from seed spilled from the bird feeders. Vervain glimmers like a slow-burning sparkler. Marzipan-scented winter heliotrope is out for Christmas. By March, grape hyacinths are studding the leaf rosettes of storksbill. The whole geranium family is a gravel speciality, with self-sown hybrids of meadow cranesbill sporting watercolour streaks and splashes, and herb robert providing the indigenous background chorus. I struggle to differentiate the geranium arrivals – cut-leaved, small-leaved, shining – which all have similar flowers and lobed leaves and are hugely variable. The most striking is the lilac hedgerow cranesbill, *Geranium pyrenaicum*, from southern Europe, which was first recorded locally as a garden escape in nearby Beccles in 1805. In our garden it began in the gravel and hopped into the meadow. It's a very adaptable plant. In patches of short mown grass it will become dwarfed, and flower an inch above the turf. In long grass and among the jostling perennials of the Mediterranean bed it turns into a climber.

But the gravel's star is the sheaf of red valerian from the Mediterranean, which basks in the warm gusts from the boiler outlet. This exuberant species with its blowsy bushels of deep pink flowers arrived in English gardens in the sixteenth century. In its home range it grows naturally on rocks and cliffs, and quickly took to stone walls in the coastal areas of the West Country. It picked up a tally of local names that sound as if they'd been lifted from seaside postcards: Drunken Sailor, Kiss-Me-Quick, Saucy Bet. It reached the austere stonework of Portland prison in Dorset, where it was dubbed Convict Grass, and eventually fetched up in East Anglia on the walls of Leiston Abbey in 1836. Monks' Comfort, perhaps. Our patch leans against the house wall in what is essentially a sauna of boiler steam. During hot weather it is the haunt of hummingbird hawk-moths (also migrants from the south) sometimes three or four at once. If we have guests for lunch outside, we turn the chairs round to watch them and whoop and gasp at their prodigious aerobatics. Their inch-long probosces, probing deep into the valerian corollas for nectar, are visible yards away, and as they hover, wings just a blur, they seem to be performing elaborate arabesques around this frontal appendage. Then they suddenly bounce away, maybe five feet into the air, as if the flower has thrust them out. They hover, dart this way and that, drop back to sip nectar again. All these manoeuvres, the swoops, the slip-sliding, the pinpoint hovering, are controlled by a tiny cluster of specialist cells halfway up the moth's antennae. It's an astounding mechanism, but no more than I would expect given the intricate lifeways of the insect world. What delights me more about the hawk-moths is the profligacy of their flying. Half their showy to-ing and fro-ing seems pointless, a waste of energy when they could just slip from flower to flower. I prefer to think that at some level they enjoy their workouts in the sun. I wonder what John Keats, a stern opponent of the work ethic, would have made of them. He wrote to his friend John Reynolds, then housebound by chronic illness: 'Now it is more noble to sit like Jove than to fly like Mercury – let us not therefore go hurrying about and collecting honey, bee-like buzzing here and there impatiently from a knowledge of what is to be aimed at; but let us open our leaves like a flower and be passive and receptive …'

Fortunately, none of our visitors have so far evolved into nuisances, either in our garden or the surrounding countryside. But some immigrant species have become notorious for the trouble they cause. Japanese knotweed's labyrinthine root system can stop work on construction sites. Indian balsam crowds out native species along riverbanks and escaped (or dumped) aquarium plants can choke whole waterways. Species introduced from other parts of the globe and then naturalised in the wild don't bring with them the insects and diseases that keep them in check in their homelands. They're not party to the chemical negotiations that indigenous species have built up with their neighbours.

So it's sensible to be vigilant about any foreign species passing over the boundary between cultivation and the wild. Yet plants have been doing this for thousands of years, and mostly assimilating into the native vegetation without any problems. Just over half of the 3,500 plant species growing wild in the UK were originally introduced here by human agency, either deliberately or accidentally. They include familiar species like field poppy (from southern Europe, via Neolithic farmers), snowdrop (from central Europe, by medieval monks) and horse chestnut (from the Balkans, by a sixteenth-century French botanist, and possibly also by Romanies). These are all much loved species and regarded as 'honorary natives'. They're naturalised in every sense of the word.

But language is slippery here. The terms used to describe many other introduced species – 'aliens', 'invasive non-natives' – echo the intolerant language currently used about human migrants. 'Naturalisation', by contrast, seems a value-free word but carries a lot of moral baggage. In the strict scientific sense it describes the process through which an organism from elsewhere fetches up in new geographical situation and is able to survive and reproduce itself. A more general dictionary definition is 'to be admitted to the rights and privileges of a native born subject or citizen'. Unlike the scientific definition, this (though obviously phrased for humans) suggests that naturalisation is a reciprocal process, and that to be fully naturalised the newcomer must be accepted by its new neighbours. Some immigrant and introduced plants settle in and become vigorous reproducers, but are not welcome in either the human or wild communities they've colonised. Others behave as if they are just latecomers in the long process of natural colonisation. There are two out-of-place species edging ever closer to our garden that illustrate the different faces of naturalisation. They're about a quarter of a mile away at present, but will arrive in our verge eventually. Alexanders, *Smyrnium olustratum*, was introduced to Britain by the Romans as a medicine and pot-herb. It's an attractive plant, with bright green over-wintering foliage and yellow umbels that are the first wayside blooms of the spring. I tested its culinary reputation when I was writing my first book (*Food for Free*), and found the young leaf-shoots, blanched by their own foliage, quite acceptable cooked like asparagus. They were touched with a subtle tang of angelica.

Alexanders is widely naturalised in coastal regions, and for the first two thousand years of its occupation didn't venture far inland. It benefits from the coast's fewer frost days, which can cut the plant back. But in the 1980s its behaviour began to change. Encouraged by warmer winters it began colonising hedgebanks and verges far from the coast, even (as in our parish) field edges some way from any road, its seed doubtless scattered and spread by mechanical verge cutters. What's ominous is the way its dense overwintering foliage blankets the ground for much of the year, smothering many other low-growing species. As global heating advances, Alexanders is likely to spread in its wake, and in the countryside become as great a challenge as Japanese knotweed is in built-up areas.

By contrast, Danish scurvy grass is a dainty, white-flowered, low growing native. It's indigenous on clifftops and the edges of saltmarshes. At much the same time as Alexanders began its expansion, Danish scurvy grass started hitchhiking inland along the trunk road system. The prostrate plants grow close together on the central reservations and bare edges of the roads, simulacra of their native habitats. In their peak flowering season in late March and April it is as if a deep and sparkling ribbon of rime has gripped the verges.

Again weather is involved, though indirectly this time. The roads colonised by the scurvy grass are almost exclusively those that have been sprayed with salt during winter ice-ups. The increased salinity of the verges suits this seashore plant, whose seeds are sucked along in the traffic's slipstream. In the last hard winter our narrow lane was salted for the first time. A year later the first mats of scurvy grass brightened what is a rather gloomy road home.

Danish scurvy grass is an annual, and more or less vanishes after flowering. It has no unneighbourly impact on human activities or other vegetation, and can be said to be fully naturalised. I call it 'Wayfrost'.

Where does a plant properly belong? Beyond their transportation by humans, plants have always been autonomous wanderers, carried by ocean currents and migrating birds, their ranges pushed this way and that by changes in the climate. But beneath this slow nomadic drift there is a compelling sense of the kind of environment into which an individual species 'fits'. This is not just an ecological fit (type of soil, shade, humidity, etc) but a cultural one, based on long associations. Plants aren't passive objects in a landscape; they help comprise and shape those landscapes, and our experience of place.

The nineteenth-century poet John Clare had a clear and precocious view of this. In a poem called 'Shadows of Taste' he expresses his disgust with scientific collectors who 'steal nature from its proper dwelling place'. He applauds instead persons 'of taste', by which he means those who appreciate wild things in their context, both natural and cultural. And then in a remarkable stanza he suggests that 'taste' is a faculty enjoyed by all living things. It's their inherited, unconscious choice of – and comfortableness in – their natural habitats. By his strikingly original use of this single word, he puts all beings on a common footing in their relationships with their 'proper dwelling place'.

> Not mind alone the instinctive mood declares
> But birds & flowers & insects are its heirs
> Taste is their joyous heritage & they
> All choose for joy in a peculiar way

Much of my own outdoor joyousness comes from experiencing organisms in their proper dwelling places, which in that moment provides me with a sense of belonging too, a feeling of shared *haunts*. It's an act of witness, often recorded, and seems to me an authentic way for a language-using species such as ourselves to relate to our fellow beings, and as ecologically valid as any kind of manipulative engagement. The novelist John Fowles, despite being a writer on nature himself and the curator of the fossil-filled Lyme Regis Museum, despised all such recordings. Words, he proclaimed, were 'a pane of smoked glass' between us and the world. In his meditation on *The Tree* he suggests that the experience of nature through 'selected image, gardened word, through other eyes and minds, betrays or banishes its reality.' I knew Fowles slightly and always disagreed with him on this. Our recorded acts of witness seem to me as natural for us as scent-marking by foxes.

Ronald Blythe, writing of his Suffolk boyhood, remembers the time when village people of all ages saw wild plant colonies 'as a form of permanent geography, by which the distance of Sunday walks could be measured, or where tea or love could be made.' There's less permanence about their geography now, and the changes as well as the continuity of floral landscapes and parochial customs are recorded in that bulwark of botanical literature, the local Flora. The Reverend W. Keble Martin is best known for the book which transformed popular botanical field guides in the 1960s, *The Concise British Flora in Colour*. But thirty years earlier he had masterminded the compilation of a Flora for his home county of Devon. It's a gentle, intimate volume, in which different species are logged according to their villages. He lists seven varieties of the common dog violet, including the white-flowered Forma *luxuriana* which had been found in just three parishes: Christow, Hennock, and Newton Abbot. Gilbert White was even more precise, giving full addresses for his findings. While I was writing his biography I was able to rediscover many of these plants in the exact locations White first recorded for them, including the colony of wall lettuce and hart's-tongue fern 'in a most shady part of the hollow lane under the cover of the rock as you first enter the lane ... on the right-hand side before you come to Nine-acre lane'.

I've done my mite towards a few county Floras, and relish the disciplines of search and identification involved, the growing intimacy with a habitat, the learning of plant anatomy and the unaccustomed language of awms and pedicels. Are the leaf-hairs forked? Sepals longer than

petals? Sometimes I'm at the edge of my sensory abili-
ties here, searching with my fingers for barely perceptible
downiness, sniffing for evanescent odours from seeds. It is
gratifying when you succeed in translating a plant's identity card and can talk for a moment in its own language.
This never seems like scientific commodification, more
a process of genuine acquaintanceship. Who are you?
Where do you live? When did we first become aware of
you? On a tramp up to Heathen Grove once I stumbled
on a colony of the jewel-like lily herb paris growing in
the runkled earth by a badger sett. I'd never seen it in my
home range before, and peered in a kind of bliss at its four
opposite leaves and crown of eight golden stamens (it's
named for its numerical harmony – *herba paris,* the herb of
parity, or 'pairs') but mostly at the sheer wonder of it being
there, in my sight, on my patch. Back home I looked it up
in a Hertfordshire Flora from 1849. It had been recorded
in 'Great Berkhampstead ... Near Ashlyns', by none other
than Augustus Smith, the radical squire who had helped
engineer the liberation of our common. Heathen Grove
was part of Smith's Ashlyns estate, and though it's highly
unlikely I had found paris on the same spot as him, it is a
wanderer in its favoured haunts, and could well have been
a descendant. I'd count this as just two degrees of separation from one of my heroes.

Records like this map the most intimate grain of
vegetation. They're accounts of an encounter between
individual plants and particular humans in a specific place.
The plant of course knows nothing of this, but the record
is a message sent on its behalf, that it was here, and was

noticed. It is a virtual ecological link, causing effects over time in how it is viewed and treated.

How does this play out for the defining plants of our home patch in Norfolk? I have personal favourites, landmarks on strolls, flashes of seasonal colour that tell me I'm close to home. The heath known as the Ling, our gateway from the south, is rust-red in July from mats of sheep's sorrel, then lilac from August heather. Closer home, a hundred yards from our house, a road-island is blanketed with red dead-nettle in March and with candy-striped field bind-weed in July. By the side of the lane that strikes north from this island is a ditch where I always look for the first cel-andines of the year, in flower with luck for my birthday in late February (though I once forced some out with a sun-lamp for Valentine's Day).

These are personal familiars, common plants that don't have particular Norfolk connections. But there are local specialities which grow nowhere else and create unique micro-landscapes. Sulphur clover, with its bushels of straw-coloured flowers, is pretty much confined to the chalky clays of East Anglia. I know it from a dozen or so local road verges, where it blooms just after the cow-slips and gives its home patches a special savour of fading ochre. It was once locally common on unimproved grass-land, but since so much of this has vanished it's retreated to these marginal habitats. They're places of annual pil-grimage for me.

Hoary mullein is dramatically different. It's a spectac-ular, expansive plant, up to a metre and a half tall, with felted grey leaves and candelabras of bright yellow flowers. It grows chiefly in south-west Europe and is on the very edge of its range in England. Its original UK colonies were on the shingle beaches of north-west Norfolk, but judging from the early records in the eighteenth century it had already spread east along the river and road networks, colonising stony quarries and dry banks. Today its most spectacular population is on the south-facing bank of the A47 near Norwich, now one of Norfolk's great botanical landmarks. We drive past this colony regularly on our way to the Broads, and through late winter and spring it's like watching a nail-biting film trailer. In a mild winter there are thousands of overwintering silvery leaf rosettes. Hard frosts can cut them back alarmingly, reminding you of its southern origins. But in late June and July they're back again, and we drive past a mile of golden forked sceptres, cheering from the car.

These are both scarce, highly distinctive local species, so why don't I give them sanctuary in the garden? I'm not sure I have a consistent answer any longer. I know that the mantra of authenticity, which stalks me like an evangelical Puritan, has something to do with it. All those millennia of the plants' settling in and adjusting to local soils, negotiating with their neighbours, holding their ground – what does that count for if I can fabricate a colony in a year or two with a handful of plundered seed? Somewhere deep I feel that a facsimile of this kind would diminish the meaning, the specialness of those aboriginal colonies. Am I being irrational here? Both the clover and the mullein have already taken to man-made marginal habitats. Why not give them a nudge, and a boost to their survival, by introducing them to a local garden?

The difference is that the plants in the original wild colonies arrived there of their own accord. The embankments of the A47 dual carriageway may be one of the most contrived habitats in Norfolk, but at least the mulleins got there without planning or planting or any kind of deliberate human assistance. This sense of self-sufficiency, of genuine nativeness, is regarded by many as not just an ecological virtue but a moral one.

I remember the passionate arguments about the provenance of snake's-head fritillary when I was compiling *Flora Britannica* in the 1990s. The fritillary is our most darkly glamorous wildflower, its hanging bells chequered with mulberry and lilac patches which seem to overlap as if they were scales. Up until the Second World War it was quite widespread in damp meadows in southern and eastern England, before drainage and ploughing reduced it to just a handful of sites. A few of these are in meadows not far from our house. Their distribution along Suffolk river valleys and the Thames catchment area suggest they might be relics of a continuous population which, before the North Sea had opened, had occupied joined flood-plains from the Rhine to the Windrush. I wasn't the only one to fervently wish the fritillary was a naturally and anciently established European in our parishes.

Against this view was the possibility that the fritillary was a naturalised garden escape. The first British record was not until 1736, in Middlesex. The second, forty years later, was in a Suffolk meadow just twelve miles east of us. Geoffrey Grigson, the writer whose *The Englishman's Flora* made me look at plants in a new way, was one of those who argued that it was inconceivable that a such a conspicuous flower could have grown in the wild without attracting the attention of two centuries of active botanists. It was popular in big gardens in the sixteenth and seventeenth centuries (John Gerard mentions it in his *Herball*), and Grigson believed that the plant spread out from these sources by seed and bulblet. It turns out he was almost certainly right. DNA analysis has shown that the genetic profile of 'wild' English fritillaries is much closer to that of garden varieties than to the populations growing in the wild in northern Europe. The fritillary's story in the UK has come full circle. It began in the garden, hopped over the wall into damp meadows and commons, declined as these were destroyed, and has become so rare that almost all its habitats are protected, as if it were an unimpeachable native. Now it is increasingly popular in gardens again, planted up in wild flower meadows and orchards. Doubtless it will escape and the whole diaspora will begin again.

Does the provenance of the fritillary, and plants with a similar history, really matter? As the years pass and the refugees settle in, the signs of human manipulation begin to fade. Both human and natural communities begin to behave towards them as if they were long-established natives. As Peter Marren has written: 'What we do know is that these are plants that grow in harmony with native species, and that they are loved and valued, and that we would be sorry to see them vanish. By any measure of the human heart they matter.' In a time of great environmental instability, maybe we need to adopt a more generous and inclusive idea of nativeness, a more welcoming attitude towards newcomers. Our long-term inhabitants are being shifted by climate change and sometimes destroyed by the diseases proliferating in its wake. Unless we allow – even enable – new colonists in old places we could end up with impoverished ecosystems and landscapes. They are, at the very least, an insurance policy.

So, I've changed my mind. Next summer I'll gather sulphur clover seed and bring it back to plant in the short grass by the meadow, in the moderately confident belief that it may have once grown on our patch of land.

7

ABROAD

I'm increasingly conscious of my double standards in the matter of translocating plants. In another part of the garden, only feet away from the indigenous swathes of the meadow, I've built up a collection of wild species a thousand miles from their native home. I've always relished the power of plants to take you to other times and places, to *transport* you. They're mordants, fixers of experience. In the gloom of winter, and then again in the often maddeningly erratic progress of the English spring, there are moments when I long, disloyally, for wild thyme underfoot, for the blissfully unlikely sight of gladioli growing wild, for cistus and sage and rosemary bushes dotting hot limestone rocks somewhere in the south. In *The Wild Garden*, William Robinson remarked that 'the true garden ... gives us the living things themselves and not merely representations of them'. I'm not sure all garden designers regard plants as 'the living things themselves' so much as themed building blocks. But I don't think Robinson is quite right either. Plants in gardens *are* representational. They carry with them memories of childhood dens, of the path to the front door of your first house, of the dazzle and aromas of foreign holidays.

Geoffrey Grigson believed that seeing familiar wild plants in unfamiliar places could change their meaning. To encounter a pomegranate growing in a Spanish hedge is a revelation for any northern soul. Grigson was thinking especially of species that are rare, or peculiarly local, suddenly witnessed in their thousands in a southern meadow. His epiphany was the sight of bunches of lily of the valley being sold by the roadside in France, 'picked from woods where they are as thick as wood anemones ...' 'Going abroad' he continued, 'can jolt our ideas of the proper keepings or whereabouts' of plants. I'm intrigued by Grigson's use of the word 'keepings'. I think he's suggesting both 'those kept company with' and 'in keeping with' – meaning fit, appropriate, at home, something analogous to John Clare's vision of plants' 'taste'. I think a similar renewal can happen when familiar garden plants are seen in their native setting, or when a familiar foreign species is introduced to the garden. Maybe its 'keepings' are transported along with the plant itself.

One species which jolts my ideas of proper whereabouts, as well as providing a metaphor for the mischievousness of our garden, is the Mediterranean spurge, *Euphorbia characias*. Its sheaves of stalks carry frills of grey-green leaves made glaucous by tiny hairs. The flowers are held inside what look like miniature lemon-tinted satellite dishes, and light up like beacons in the sun. They adorn hillsides and pastures across the Mediterranean, and brighten our garden from late February to June, and then again sometimes in the autumn. I put in a single plant nearly two decades ago, and its descendants now ramp about at will.

A sizeable clump has set itself up among the bearded irises in our herbaceous border. More jostle their way through tangles of everlasting pea in the gravel. This year I found a spray flouncing among the dog violets in the wood. It looked thoroughly at home, the greyish leaves and citrus flowers seeming part of the pastel spectrum of the spring, and not a trespasser at all. They turn this patch of eastern England into an outpost of the Cretan hillside where I first saw them in the late 1980s.

It had been my first trip away from the UK for two decades, an escape from a long cocooning at home, locked down by a timidity I still don't properly understand. Crete bundled me out of my knowledge and into the vivid openness of the Mediterranean. What was strange to me was how *un*-foreign it all seemed. Perhaps Mediterranean culture is now more deeply embedded with us than we realise. But its limestone landscapes sounded echoes in me. They had something of the quality of chalk country I'd grown up in: a frankness, a sense of tactility and flux (Auden's 'rock which responds'). And that simple primal fact of sun shining on white stone. On that first trip I'd travelled with a party to the north coast not far from Heraklion, and part of our mission was to talk up the value of eco-tourism to the region. Crete doesn't have much in the way of planning law, and many of the coastal lagoons and marshes were vanishing under rubbish tips and speculative development. But it was clear from our first strolls on the foreshore by our hotel that the island was a sanctum of fabulous plants. We found squirting cucumber, whose gherkin-like fruits explode when they're ripe, scattering the seeds metres away. And the philosophically intriguing spiny burnet, which sports a network of protective twiggery like a sheet of chicken wire. The angles of the twigs form half hexagons, so that the whole plant looks like a vegetable honeycomb. Why this exquisite pattern? Why not an illegible tangle of random thorns? I wondered fancifully if the honeycomb was a lure for homesick bees as well as a barrier against hungry goats.

Much of the vegetation seemed to be spiny, hostile, resinous, armed with oil-skinned leaves and bristling branches, protectives against the sun and browsing animals. But we saw gracious plants too, redolent of Crete's history as an ancient island. More than 150 of Crete's native species – some 10 per cent – are endemic, and grow nowhere else on Earth. We saw endemic tulips up on the Omalos plateau, and an endemic 'weed' tulip in the arable fields below. *Tulipa doerfleri* seems to have evolved uniquely on the island since agriculture arrived here seven thousand years ago. It has fierce scarlet flowers with black beauty spots at the base of the petals, and I watched a woman gathering these wild, ornate bouquets for market. High up in the mountains there were bleached cypress trees, some over a thousand years old, their roots flowing down cliffs and the lips of gorges like lava streams. And hills everywhere were cloaked with the lemon-yellow of euphorbias and asphodel.

The following spring I made it to the south of France for the first time for twenty years. This was almost an accident itself. I'd planned a spell in the Pyrenees with my old walking chum and then literary agent Richard Simon, but we'd been driven back by late snow, and ended up on the coast near Perpignan. We spent days wandering among the rosemary and cistus, puzzling over orchid identities and watching bee-eaters hawking over a scrubland echoing with nightingale song. And I began to learn a little about the grammar of the Mediterranean flora. How it is adapted to heat and drought. How the volatile aromatics in the leaves act as a protective layer, cooling the leaves and helping to slow down water loss, just as their grey and silver colouration reflects the sun's heat. And how it is dynamic. The low growing community – thymes, lavenders, rock roses – is called *garrigue*. It's gradually infiltrated by taller evergreen shrubs – juniper, bay, broom, arbutus, mastic. When this community reaches more than a couple of metres high it's described as *maquis*. Eventually forest trees may move in, but often the maquis is cut back by fires, and the whole process of succession starts again.

A belief still persists that the Mediterranean was once blanketed by high forest, and that what remains is degraded, a 'ruined landscape' as it's been called. But buried pollen remains show that garrigue and maquis have always been abundantly present and perfectly natural habitats in regions of frequent fire. In recent years, increasing drought and changes in cultivation are causing the old olive groves and terraces to be abandoned and the area of scrub, the natural healer of broken land, is spreading. It is a bitter-sweet change, this loss of ancient practices, but it's creating a new kind of crop for the south.

I went to the south of France most years after that, often to the limestone hills and gorges of the Cevennes.

Some friends worked there as wildlife guides at a camp site and I became a devotee of the evening plant salon. We'd sit outside in the low sun with a bottle of wine and a pile of field guides. And with our ragged sheaves of leaves and flowers spread out on the table, we'd swap opinions and stories and botanical in-jokes. They were the happiest of gatherings, full of wordplay (we dubbed the hybrid between man and monkey orchid 'the missing link', but doubt we were the first). Their sociability meant they had touch of evenings in the garden about them. Our name games and lamentable jokes were just a kind of play. The swifts did their territorial dusk flights above, and below we mapped our playground with real and fantastical landmarks.

It was a trip to the Luberon in Provence that finally built a bridge for me between the wild and the garden. I'd gone with Richard Simon again, and for days we'd explored what is the French equivalent of a National Park. Stretching along the western ridge is a forest of Atlas cedars. They'd been native to Provence twenty thousand years ago, and had recently been re-introduced from Morocco – *par eaux*, the notice-boards explained mysteriously. (I recalled that a cedar had been bought to my old Oxford college on a seaborn raft). Presumably they'd been planted, but they were already surrounded by their own seedlings and a host of attendant fungi.

Below the cedars there was a south-facing hillside. The maquis of box and cistus gave way to haze of grape hyacinths and jonquils. As we climbed the narrow hill track, up to our knees in wild thyme, we realised that there were smaller delicacies in the shorter grass: clumps of star-flowered yellow tulips, tufts of what had become my favourite southern flower, blue aphyllanthes (*Aphyllanthes monspeliensis*), an almost leafless lily whose flowers are carried on stems that resemble rushes. What a symbol of the paradoxes of this arid and fiery region: a pillow of blossom borne on a bundle of spills. Then the irises began. They were *Iris chamaeri*, short-stemmed, the flowers a kaleidoscope of mauves and blues, folded like an exercise in petal origami. Some, striated with a deep Tyrian purple, had the scent of Florentine irises. But that perfume was commonplace compared to the piercing aroma of jasmine from the slender, grassy-leaved buttercup next to them. A scented buttercup! A tufted lily! I wanted to take them home, together with the whole fantastic, spontaneous rock garden they stood in.

There were raised eyebrows among my friends when I first announced plans for a Mediterranean garden. They regarded it as an alarming descent into herbaceous convention for a self-styled wild thing. Or, at best, an inexorable route to tedium and disappointment: 'three weeks of colour in June, and then the whole lot massacred by frost'. I should have explained more clearly what I had in mind – which wasn't some eclectic dry garden, with ornamentals from South Africa and California. Of course, I hoped to create a patch that was attractive and floriferous and would tolerate our increasing summer heat and drought. But what I really dreamed of was a time capsule – or more accurately a space-time capsule – of all those adventures in the landscapes of the south, now increasingly difficult for me to reach in person. And true to the spirit of the garden, I wanted to devote it to wild species, and see if I could forge a rough replica of Mediterranean vegetation.

Its destined site was the large oval bed that had once contained the azaleas and hebes. All it needed was a radical change in the character of the soil, a neutralising of its acid aftertaste. By a stroke of luck our garden helper Ray – always savvy about my schemes – had heard that a load of limestone rubble from a quarry in Lincolnshire had arrived in the village as ballast for a lorry. A few hours later it was on our drive and being ferried to the burgeoning bed. I salved my ecological conscience with the thought that it was almost local and was being recycled, having already been dug from the ground. Over the weeks that followed I scrumped flint stones from the local fields, and used them to build up miniature terraces and hummocks.

Then I began planting. I wanted a mix of garrigue and maquis, a scatter of aromatic shrubs interspersed with low-growing herbs and bulbs. The framework of sage and lavender and bay and rosemary was easy, and I bought it off-the-peg at the local garden centre. Beyond that I wanted plants I'd experienced in the wild myself, the companions I yearned for in dull English weather, and that meant months of searching in specialist nurseries. When I found a source for the little blue aphyllanthes from Provence with its quills of azure starflowers, it had pride of place on one of my hummocks. I tracked down some of the totemic species I'd seen on Crete, the cornfield tulip, the pink *Cistus creticus,* and of course, that ebullient euphorbia. Nursery labelling of the scarcer species proved erratic. Supposed Corsican crocuses turned out to be municipal bedding varieties, and what was advertised as a rare Greek *Lithodora* arrived as a West Country gromwell. But I was able to track down the scented buttercup from the Luberon, and a yellow asphodel. And against the odds, add a real tang of southern Spain; I'd gathered a pocketful of seed from some dried-out plants on an Andalusian roadside the summer before, and sown them in a tray. Remarkably some of them germinated and thrived – a Spanish broom, an unidentifiable cistus, a wild rose with startling black hips, an annual *Echinops*.

And confounding all the sceptics, the garrigue flowered not just for three weeks but for three months, in a blaze of pastel colours and delirious butterflies. Its residents spurned watering and manuring. The sages and rosemaries went on flowering right into November. The Algerian iris was in bloom on Christmas day. Even during the freeze-ups of their first winter, these desert plants stood their ground, their downy leaves catching the frost so they glittered like tinsel in the early mornings. Two of the tenderest lavenders were cut back, but when snow piled up over one of them and formed a kind of igloo, a charm of goldfinches edged inside and shredded the seeds in a cloud of violet chaff.

In the years that followed I added new species as I found them: a myrtle, a Florentine iris in palest blue, a rather fetching two-toned grape hyacinth from Turkey. Beyond these plantings, I let the Med bed develop as it wished. I wanted the shrubs to spread their wings, and the ground plants to set their seed. Which they duly did. The juniper topped three metres and met the Jerusalem sage in a bushy embrace. The marjoram and euphorbia began to crowd out the tulips. Inexorably, what was garrigue turned into maquis. The deep-rooted fertility of the old azalea bed still lurked. And added to the nitrogen-heavy English rain it was making everything grow larger and faster and more thuggish than it would have done in the arid soils of the Mediterranean. Many of the low-growing species, like my beloved aphyllanthes, simply died from overshading or over-nourishment. Then our garden endemic, ground elder (which Polly demonises as 'grelda'), moved in and proved as ineradicable as it is in other parts of the garden. Following my own philosophy, I let it all happen, hoping forlornly that the result might be a new vegetational hybrid, some harmonious Anglo-Grecian shrubbery. But it didn't. The foliage just closed up, and became a com-pacted mass of twiggery and grelda, too dense for my fading flexibility to tackle.

But again chance came to the rescue. We were having tea at a friend's cottage in the next village where the view was that Norfolk rarity – a glimpse through the trees of a little valley, a strange echo of my primal teenage view across the winterbourne and up to Heathen Grove. Almost simultaneously I had a vivid memory of the prospect from a courtyard in Crete, and began to glimpse a possible solu-tion to the illegible tangle. I imagined two winding paths, cut through the bushes and surfaced with limestone chips. And I saw that this would not only open up views of the wild garden beyond, but give me a chance to get among the bushes and keep them marginally in check. A few weeks later, Ray came in with his heavy machinery and did the job perfectly. And we were charmed and tickled by the result. From the patio we could see right through the clear trunks of the big cistuses and across the meadow cowslips to the wood. The golden euphorbias shone against the white limestone. It all looked, I was pleased to see, positively Cretan.

8

GENIUS LOCI

A view across our garden in late spring reveals a scene of such luxuriance that a stranger might diagnose abandonment, or at least incorrigible neglect. Everywhere wild and cultivated plants co-habit, as do wild and cultivated ambitions. The white haze of cow parsley embroiders every patch of green. In Polly's walled vegetable garden, opium poppies are erupting through the lettuces. Cornflowers edge her curvaceous potato rows. Nearer the house roses are not so much climbing romantically around the front door as butting through it. What was a beech hedge is now an ivy hedge (wonderful for bees when it's in flower). Oaklings are peeking through the flowering currants. Every aspiring sharp edge frays into a fringe, with grass, flower, even the soil itself all mutually overlaid and interwoven. If we'd moved in when we were twenty years younger I guess we might have organised it more, laid out hedged paths and compartments, differentiated the spaces, gone for the outside room approach. But a designed garden, even a naturalistically inclined one, is not really to either of our tastes or skills, and we sympathise with Geoffrey Grigson's view of such picturesque plots. 'I walk around such gardens and see them only as canvases, and would never be surprised if a tractor came trundling in, loaded with gigantic gilt frames which would be disposed here and there among the trees and the temples.'

The idea of a 'naturalistic garden' has always been something of a confidence trick, a sleight of hand whereby earth and plants are arranged to mimic supposed natural formations, with soft lines and tasteful alternations of grass, water and tree – though as Grigson hints, the real models were the mythic landscapes of seventeenth- and eighteenth-century paintings. Most have been heavily manipulated, and in their evolutionary past were driven by an ideological belief that nature was flawed, no more than a rough sketch. It needed 'Improvement' to achieve harmony and perfection. Horace Walpole, eighteenth-century aesthete and philosopher of Improvement, wrote that 'the living landscape must be chastened and polished'. Nature must be 'rescued and improved', the damage of the Fall made good. Landscape designers like Capability Brown took all this literally, levelling houses that spoilt the view, diverting unruly watercourses, planting neat clumps of trees like woodland canapes, banishing the scruffy, scrubby natural transition zone between grass and tree. Alexander Pope's famous instruction to landscapers to 'consult the genius of the place' – e.g. echo local landforms and vegetation – in practice meant subcontracting to the 'genius' of earth-movers like Brown.

One summer I went to an exhibition at our county museum in Norwich Castle by the French artist, Hubert Duprat, entitled 'Caddis, Crystal and Company'. Duprat is known for his whimsical manipulations of natural objects and the questions they raise about art and beauty. One playful exhibit was a series of flints painstakingly chipped and arranged into the rough silhouettes of swans' necks and dogs' heads such as those made by casting the shadow of your hand on a wall. The catalogue suggested the work referenced Mediterranean cave art and Norfolk flint-knapping. To me it chiefly tagged an engaging kids' game.

The headline piece in the show was small aquarium containing caddis-fly larvae, whose cocoons were decked out with gold leaf and pearls and what looked like fragments of gemstones. The larvae, shrimp-like animals that live on the bottom of streams and lakes, build protective cases for their time underwater. They're made from silk secreted from their salivary glands and reinforced by foraged bric-a-brac – grains of sand and gravel, fragments of bark, leaves and seeds, even flakes of mollusc shells – all carefully arranged and stuck on to the surface of the silken cocoon. Each genus of caddis fly has its own favoured materials and style of construction. I saw these bejewelled versions before I'd read the catalogue, and was mildly shocked. It looked as if the larvae had been manually ornamented while still alive, a possibility that reminded me of the obscene practice in some fashionable circles of using tethered live beetles as jewellery.

But then I watched the video of how the trick was done. Duprat had replaced the mundane riverbed debris that is the caddis fly's usual raw material with his sparkling gems and gewgaws, and the insects had then assembled them into fantastical overcoats. This posed an intriguing question. Who was the artist: Duprat or the caddis fly? According to Guillaume Desanges, the French authority on Duprat's work, the answer is straightforward. Echoing Horace Walpole and an entire tradition of humanist aesthetics, he makes a grand assertion about natural beauty: 'it is strictly and precisely within the field of art that natural phenomena take on meaning ... it is not nature which is beautiful but its submission to art.' I imagine the caddis fly, which after all has to make the final decision about how to arrange the maestro's *objets trouvés,* might have something to say about this.

It's a moot point whether the caddis fly has an aesthetic sense guiding its shell-building decisions. I'm inclined to think some other beings do, given the sheer unnecessary extravagance of the things they create. I've seen a goldfinch's nest ornamented with garlands of forget-me-nots. The red kites in the Chilterns are notorious for gathering bits of ornamental underwear from washing lines to decorate their nests. And nightingales have a repertoire of up to two hundred phrases from which they improvise their enchanting songs. Do these emerge much like a randomised playlist from a computer? Or does the bird make deliberate choices? And if so, on what basis?

It's intriguing that our species can find such natural artefacts pleasing. But Desanges's contention that they need 'submission to art' to make them 'beautiful' is preposterous. Some thinkers have argued that there are intrinsic qualities in the natural world that form an abstract calculus of beauty. Symmetry is one such, and perhaps the most absurd. No life form is perfectly

symmetrical. Oddity and imperfection are the character-
istics of all living things, and one way of telling them
from engineered replicas. Lewis Thomas, in his essay
'The Wonderful Mistake' wrote that 'Biology needs a
better word than "error" for the driving force in evolution. Or maybe "error" will do after all, when you
remember that it came from an old root meaning to
wander about, looking for something.' Corporeal ratios
that correspond to some 'golden section' are another
candidate in the beauty contest. John Ruskin thought
that the proportions of the water plantain, *Alisma plan-
tago-aquatica*, were the type of Divine beauty itself. 'If
the reader will take the trouble to measure the lengths
[of the ascending flower-stalks] and compare them he
will find that ... the uppermost AE = 5/7 of AD, AD =
6/8 of AC, and AC = 7/9 of AB; a most subtle dimin-
ishing proportion' and 'typical of that unity which we
attribute to God'. Water plantain grows in a pond on the
green a few hundred yards from our garden. It has tiny
three-petalled blooms, striated with pink, at the end of
flower stalks that radiate from the main stem in whorls.
The whorls diminish in diameter the closer they are to
the tip of the plant, giving the whole ensemble the look
of an old-fashioned wireless mast. I've taken a ruler to it
and the plant is elegant, in a minor key sort of way. But
in terms of commonly accepted notions of beauty it's
not a patch on the yellow flags that grow next to it. I'd
go along with the 'ordinary language use' view of my
old philosophy tutor. Beauty, as an idea, is human-de-
fined. We decide what deserves the tag, guided by social

and cultural conventions, personal experience and the emotion of the moment. It may be a view of skyscrapers, a vivid colour, a human hand, a vintage wine, a smart joke, an act of kindness, a caddis fly's exquisitely sculptured shell. 'Submission to art' has nothing to do with it. So copious are the experiences labelled 'beautiful' that I wonder if it's a considered judgement at all, and not more of a visceral exclamation, a sophisticated version of 'Wow!'. In April 2022, a patch of our meadow cowslips and blue-flowered ground ivy bloomed together in tight formation, as usual. But this spring they were the colours of the Ukrainian flag, which stopped me in my tracks. There is no such thing as an abstract dissociated view. Everything we see is in a specific place and time, and experienced through the lens of all our remembered experience.

But might there be a form of beauty in nature outside human taste and judgement? The fact perhaps that it all works and fits together so perfectly? At one level everything is beautiful, simply from the deeply improbable fact of existing. And as for living organisms and living processes – is there a single one that doesn't ripple your mind with astonishment when you consider it? Charles Darwin concluded *On the Origin of Species* with a heart-stirring paean to the elegance of being: 'from so simple a beginning endless forms most beautiful and most wonderful have evolved and are being evolved.'

In the autumn of 2020, the endless forms of bush and tree in the garden were all draped with fruit. The blackberries were ripe and bursting by late July. Falling acorns were rattling off the car roof. The weight of fruit on our trees was breaking branches, and one wilding had collapsed in on itself. It looked like a tent made of apples. As for our cherries, our beloved mazzards, it was the first year we harvested as many as the blackbirds. Spoilt by their plentifulness I had a stab at making cherry clafoutis, three different ways.

Curiously, many of the cherry leaves had withered, and curled up into what resembled green cigars. I wasn't too worried, imagining it was probably some minor infection of purely cosmetic concern. I was intrigued that these apparently ruined leaves were proving a magnet for bumble bees, which seemed to be feeding on or in them. I consulted my learned friend the writer and broadcaster Brett Westwood, and he diagnosed cherry aphid, *Myzus cerasi,* an insect specific to cherry, whose honeydew excretions were being used as a source of sugar by the bees. I uncurled some of the leaves, and sure enough there were the tiny black insects, sucking sap. I loved the idea that evolution had thrown up a species as exclusively addicted to cherry trees as I was that week.

But there was more. Inside the rolled leaves there were also ladybird larvae, feeding on the aphids, and sooty moulds colonising the honeydew. It was a whole ecosystem in miniature: leaf feeding aphid, aphids' honeydew feeding bumble bee; fungal mould and ladybird feeding on aphid, bee pollinating next year's cherry blossom, the resultant fruit feeding blackbirds – and us. Most beautiful and wonderful! I thought how close I had come to casually snipping off these curled, darkening leaves with their intricate cargo, for no better reason than that they seemed to be visually disfigured.

9

ROSE-TINTED

I'm writing this in my library as a more conventional source of garden beauty is slowly blocking out the light. A shrub rose called Etoile d'Hollande is fanning out across the downstairs windows and tiptoeing up to the bedrooms. It has deep vermilion flowers and a voluptuous vinous scent. It was bred in Holland a century ago and is always the first of our roses to come into bloom, sometimes in late April. By June, the fanfare of aroma and colour that is the mayfly glory of old roses is rolling right round the garden: Fantin Latour, Willie Lobb, Omar Khayyam, the White Rose of York, Gloire de Dijon, Rambling Rector, Rosa Mundi, Apothecary's Rose ... their names echoing a millenium of devotion in vicarage gardens and French perfumeries and pedants' libraries. And thinking of them beside the hay rattle's parasitism and the bush cricket's grate, I wonder briefly if their elegant presence here is a category error, whether they are really a kind of weed, 'a plant in the wrong place'. But they're big, shaggy, enticing bushes now. They straggle over walls and trellises with fringes of bladder campion and hedge-bedstraw twined with their lower branches. They

2

show traces of deer browse lines and seem utterly part of our feral landscape.

My dad grew a lot of roses in our Chiltern garden, mostly tea roses and modern hybrids. But there was one bloom that stood out. My school's Founder's Day was held in the middle of June, and it was the custom to wear a red rose buttonhole in honour of the Tudor founder. I knew exactly which of my dad's roses to pick: a ruby scrolled bloom with a deep, slightly intoxicating perfume, and held on a long stem just right for a blazer lapel. I don't know for sure what variety it was, but I like to imagine it was what was popularly known as General Jack (short for General Jacqueminot), one of the varieties originating in France in the nineteenth-century heyday of rose breeding. As we gathered in the quad, I puffed out my chest, adorned with what I was sure was the smartest rose there.

My other childhood engagements with garden roses were more basic, and in tune with my hunter-gatherer's life in the Field. I made a pulp with the petals, crammed and pounded with a little water, and used it as a rough jam or primitive perfume. After that my attention was pretty much confined to the wild dog rose, and its various manifestations in folk cookery. But that changed in 1982 when I helped make a television series entitled *Back to the Roots*. Its subject was the current revival of old plant varieties and growing traditions. In a programme on lost flowers we visited Lime Kiln, Humphrey Brooke's famous rose garden in Claydon, Suffolk (not many miles from where Polly and I live now). Brooke was a distinguished art historian and curator, deputy director of the Tate Gallery and Secretary to the Royal Academy. In the 1970s, the onset of bipolar syndrome caused his early retirement to Lime Kiln, a medieval house owned by his wife Sophie Benckendorff's Russian family, where he devoted himself to building up the biggest collection of shrub roses in Britain. When he greeted us, chain-smoking and with crates of beer stacked up in his garage for the film crew, we suspected the day would turn out to be a lively one.

Lime Kiln's rose garden was a revelation. No tidy rows of clipped shrubs or leggy standards, but a tumult of more than five hundred sprawling, overlapping and ebulliently floriferous bushes. A visiting French journalist had commented that 'n'est ce pas une roseraie. C'est un jungle de roses.' Brooke explained that he had a taste for historic shrub roses, varieties with pedigrees going back centuries, whose short-lived single blooming was compensated by flowers of intense perfume and intricate structure. He had no time for the conventional protocols of rose growing, and never sprayed, fed or even pruned his plants, just clipped them occasionally to prevent them overwhelming each other and the garden paths from closing up. Two varieties in particular had beguiling biographies. Souvenir de la Malmaison had been bred in France in 1843 and named in honour of Empress Josephine's legendary rose garden at Château de Malmaison. Lime Kiln's specimen was a huge brambly climber, its flowers formed of densely bunched and elaborately folded petals, just touched with blush pink and carrying a sublime and subtle scent. It's one of the very few old roses that will flower more than once in a year, often deep into December, and Brooke always sent a bouquet from his own bush to the Queen Mother for Christmas Day.

Brooke had rediscovered the other variety himself, growing up against the wall of Woolverstone Church in Suffolk. It was of unknown origin but obviously an antique, and he encouraged its transition back into commercial cultivation under the name of Surpassing Beauty of Woolverstone. It is deep red and has a strong, fruity scent. He told us, on camera, that he'd invited a blind friend to smell the bloom, who'd responded by saying 'if this scent was available in a bottle it would put every tart in Europe out of business'. Rosarians can be as extravagant as wine-makers in their descriptions of perfumes, and raspberry, peppermint, cigar boxes, warm butter, musk and passion fruit have all been conjured out of different varieties. But Humphrey's friend's erotic intimation was a new one.

We took Humphrey to the local pub for lunch, an outing that involved some tricky negotiation, as he'd recently been banned for flirting with the barmaid (he was sixty-eight at the time). Later we walked him a little unsteadily back to Lime Kiln, and on the way passed a suburban front garden containing some unexceptional yellow-flowered and neatly pruned garden-centre roses. Humphrey stopped, gazed at these manifestations of everything that Lime Kiln was opposed to, and screamed 'vegetable rats!' at them and the astonished gardener, busy dead-heading.

It was a spectacular hissy-fit, and a very odd epithet for a class of roses whose worst sin is maybe having a touch of bling. But I could see what he disliked in them – their waxen petals and brash colours, and an absence of what might be called the essence of rosaceousness – that wild, unkempt, headily perfumed fandango of crumpled silk petals and tangled thorn. There's now an extreme antithesis to this, in roses developed for the cut-flower trade: perfect, pointed, odourless buds that never even open.

I could also see that a degree of snobbishness hung over the old rose cult, and that maybe I'd already unconsciously tapped into this in my struttings on the school quad. But I'd fallen for these complicated, history-laden blooms, and these were the first roses I grew for myself, and later the ones that Polly and I introduced to our new garden. I've tried to work out what captivates me about them, and why they don't seem out of place even in the most free form corners of our plot. I love their dynamism and caprice, their sense of not being quite straightforward. I'm tempted to use a favourite epithet of William Robinson's, the 'indefiniteness' which he praised as the mark of the freest and most beautiful vegetation. Robinson also had views about their disposition in a garden. They should be planted thickly, 'not thinly, like gooseberries', and the climbing varieties should be allowed to 'grace our walls ... festoon our trees, clamber up poles, or spray over the waste spaces'. He was a kindred spirit of the accidental garden. There are also the seductive pedigrees of these old varieties, the results of two thousand years of cross-breeding from dozens of species of European and middle-eastern wild roses. And then in the nineteenth century, the introduction of Chinese species, with their chrome shades and repeat flowering. The full saga of the rose dynasty is an epic narrative of social and cultural history.

We put in about thirty varieties around our garden, up against trees and walls, edging paths and spraying waste places wherever there was space. I even put one in the Mediterranean bed. *Rosa gallica* is a wild species from southern Europe with fragrant, floppy, deep-pink flowers, and is one of the most ancient ancestors of cultivated varieties. I had to have my name rose too, *R. richardii* (now *R. sancta*), the Holy Rose, whose perfectly simple single flowers in palest pink were used as a decorative motif by the Egyptians, and may have been the model for the formal carved roses in medieval churches. It possibly originated as a natural hybrid between *R. gallica* and the middle-eastern species, *R. phoenicia*. Inspiration from Lime Kiln brought us Surpassing Beauty, which flowers abundantly by the walled garden gate, but drops all its leaves by mid June, and Souvenir de la Malmaison, which now cloaks an old pear tree and has skyward ambitions. Its June flowering is problematic. The tight-bunched flowers can be reluctant to open, and in rain they turn into malodorous balls of sodden tissue. But the second flowering in autumn is different, free and fragrant and confident. Our specimen of the notorious climber Rambling Rector has great bushels of single musk-scented flowers that turn it as cream-coated as a May tree in full bloom. It has scaled a dead tree, and a few years ago its tentacles looked as if they were poised to trapeze right over the lane. Polly and I have debates about where judicious snipping becomes gratuitous pruning; on this occasion, a restraining order was the only neighbourly option.

We also have two varieties with strong local connections. The Burnet rose, *R. pimpinellifolia*, grows on sandy soils and cliffs around the Norfolk and Suffolk coast. It has creamy white flowers and what for me is the warmest and most subtle scent of all roses. When I first saw it, on the limestone pavements of the Burren in County Clare, I tried to parse its elusive aroma. I wrote down 'honey, clotted cream and jasmine', though these days a more modest use of hyperbole might make me drop the jasmine. The rose is especially connected with the heaths and crumbling cliffs of Dunwich, a Suffolk village that has been slowly collapsing into the sea since the Middle Ages. Burnet rose's resilient presence, cocking a snook at the ruins around it, generated a peerless piece of Victorian doggerel:

> '... the Dunwich Rose, with snow-like blossom
> soft, pure and white as is the cygnet's bosom ...
> which decks the stern and sterile cliff; and throws
> oe'r its rough brow new beauty where it grows ...'

Some of the Dunwich plants are markedly prostrate, have a slight yellow tinge in the petals and have been given the status of a Latinised variety: *Rosa* 'Dunwichensis'. This is the one we have planted next to Omar Khayyam, an ancient damask with ragged pink-flushed petals bunched round a yellow eye. Just how this rose travelled to our garden from a village in Persia via a charismatic Suffolk poet is a story of longing and the heavy weight of symbolism that some flowers have to bear.

Edward FitzGerald is arguably Suffolk's patron poet. He was born near Woodbridge in 1807 and moved with his wealthy family to nearby Boulge Hall in the 1830s. He was an eccentric agnostic Romantic, and chose to live away from his conformist parents in a lodge in the hall's grounds. Later he moved to Woodbridge, where he took up with a local fisherman called Posh ('beautiful like a Greek statue'). They bought a herring boat together which they dubbed *Scandal*, reputedly after Woodbridge's favourite commodity.

FitzGerald had become fascinated by eastern writings and culture when he was at Cambridge, and from 1859 began publishing a translation of the quatrains of the twelfth-century Persian astronomer-poet Omar Khayyam. Fitzgerald's version of *The Rubaiyat* was composed as a continuous sequence, and is probably best remembered today for the lines 'A Jug of Wine, a Loaf of Bread – and Thou/ Beside me singing in the Wilderness ...'. *The Rubaiyat* was a slow seller to start with, but by the 1890s had become a cult book. Pilgrims visited Omar's grave at Naishapur, and one of them, the artist and traveller William Simpson, brought back to England some hips from the pink rose growing by the tomb. (Omar had given instructions about his burial, that it 'shall be where the north wind can scatter it with rose petals'.) The seeds were propagated at Kew Gardens, seemingly grew true to their parent, and in 1893 the Omar Khayyam Society planted one of the bushes by FitzGerald's grave in Boulge churchyard on the hall's estate.

Over the years that followed, devoted disciples of both poets snipped away cuttings as souvenirs, one of them perhaps to become the progenitor of the Omar Khayyam roses now in cultivation, including our own in Norfolk. By the late 1960s, visitors to FitzGerald's grave reported finding only a stump remaining. In the early 1970s, the Shah of Persia somehow got word of this depletion, and ordered his UK ambassador to arrange the planting of *six* replacement bushes round FitzGerald's grave. It's not clear if these were cuttings from the original shrub on Omar's tomb or sourced from English-grown stock. But a grand ceremonial planting at Boulge church was set up for a November day in 1972. My friend Ronald Blythe, who lived close by, was there, along with a large contingent of the local population. He described the day to me, which turned into a classic English muddle of reverence and farce. The weather was cold and miserable. The roses had arrived but not the ambassador. Then the electricity failed and paraffin lamps and candles had to be sent for. As the congregation shivered impatiently, the rector climbed the pulpit and announced that he would take responsibility for planting the roses. At last, as he was heeling them in, a Rolls Royce bearing a Persian pennant came up the track. The ambassador disembarked, 'very tall and wearing a coat with an Astrakhan collar'. 'Oh you English,' he quipped, 'you are so *prompt*! We came Newmarket way and had lunch.' It was hardly a benediction, but at least the Omar Khayyams were in the ground.

Polly and I made a pilgrimage to Boulge one June, at the time our own Omar Khayyam was in full bloom. The hall was demolished in 1955, and finding the estate church was an adventure in itself, a journey by narrow lanes and tunnels of trees and carved wooden signposts. The churchyard was cloaked with wildflowers, as was the Gothic mausoleum of the Fitzgerald family, and we sat among the tombstones listening to the blackcaps. Edward chose not to be buried with his family, and his simple flat tombstone lies just to one side of them. But there was no sign of any of the six Omar Khayyam roses. Instead, caged inside a cylinder of chicken wire bearing the inscribed plate of the 1893 planting, was a nondescript modern rose with a single yellow flower. It had the air not of a vegetable rat but a forlorn and abandoned pet.

There are a dozen indigenous rose species in the UK (plus many sub-species, hybrids and naturalised escapees). Nine of these occur in East Anglia and three locally. The commonest, the dog rose, *R. canina*, grows wild in our garden, clambering up the ash and maple trees. It also sprouts occasionally from the rootstocks of the cultivated varieties, an oblique reminder of the whole family's wild origins.

But the best dog roses are in a lane just beyond the house. It's one of my summer pilgrimage routes. It winds through what was woodland in the Middle Ages and is lined by tall hedges and drifts of sulphur clover, and throughout June it's garlanded by dog roses in every shade from washed-out white to peach pink, some of them forming arches over the lane. The intensity of the rose-scape here always bewitches me. I remember a riddle I was taught years ago, and get drawn beyond the flowers to their bewhiskered sepals. The riddle is called 'The Five Brethren of the Rose', and is a prompt to close attention:

> *On a summer day, in sultry weather*
> *Five brethren were born together.*
> *Two had beards and two had none*
> *And the other had but half a one.*

And there through my lens I can see the answer to the riddle: two sepals with 'bearded' edges, two without, and one with whiskers down just one edge.

Nestled here and there beneath the soaring dog roses is a more understated species called the field rose, though it's more commonly associated with woodland. It's compact, with purple-tinged stems that hold the flowers close to the bush. The white blooms carry golden domes of anthers, and through my glass again I can make out the busy round bodies of pollen beetles foraging through them. Their scent is gorgeous; a cool, sweet musk, reminiscent of Rambling Rector, which isn't surprising as most scrambling and climbing rose varieties – multifloras, floribundas, musk roses – all belong to the same botanical group *(Synstylae)*. It's likely that Shakespeare had the field rose in mind in his catalogue of the seductively fragrant wildings of Titania's couch in *A Midsummer Night's Dream*:

I know a bank where the wild thyme blows,
Where oxlips and the nodding violet grows,
Quite o'er-canopied with luscious woodbine,
With sweet musk-roses and with eglantine.

It also seems to be the species in Nicholas Hilliard's famous portrait, 'Young Man among Roses', standing quite tidily beside the beruffed and lovesick youth. No wonder it has an honourable place in the breeding line of garden roses. A chance double, or a cross with *Rosa gallica*, before the fifteenth century produced the White Rose of York. Miscegenation is one of the great engines of evolution.

It's been growing for five years now, a fierce, anonymous, unaccountable rose. It sprang up in the gravel (where else), just a couple of feet from the kitchen drain. It has single white flowers that are similar to Rambling Rector's and share its musky scent, with just a tinge of added nutmeg. But there any similarity ends. The stems are vigorously upright and viciously thorny, and show no sign yet of sprawling or rambling. The leaves are elegant oblongs in dark glossy green. The flowers are bunched in racemes, beehives of more than a hundred blooms for each stalk. And just as they begin to fade away they become splashed and veined with elegiac pink. I doubt even a DNA test could establish its parentage, but I like to imagine an adventurous pollen beetle beating the bounds, dropping in on a field rose maybe or a pink-flowered American Pillar, and finally alighting to pollinate a Rambling Rector. Ancient genes are roused and mixed, and the hip that follows is eaten and excreted by a blackbird, producing this prodigy that in its final stages of flowering looks less like a rose bush than a cactus in dense bloom. Surpassing Beauty of Mazzard! I'm tempted to become a proper gardener, take cuttings and make my fortune.

Across the meadow and at the furthest possible cultural distance from the roses is a huge and sprawling gorse bush. No plant breeder to my knowledge has ever tried to 'improve' gorse, to blunt its spines or soften the glowing chrome of its flowers. It stands as a barbed and uncompromising example of a plant determined to live on its own terms; a brash, festive chancer, and a totemic species of unfenced country. Gorse usually carries a few flowers most months of the year, and there's a saying that 'when gorse is in blossom, kissing's in season'. I think there's a 'where' implicit in that 'when'. Gorse is a signature plant of commonland and rough open spaces, a vulgar plant in the precise sense, where lovers could meet and lose themselves in its perfumed thickets. I planted this bush and few others at the edge of the trees, partly because of the sense I had of encouraging a patch of simulated commonland.

It's been a signature plant for me too, of home landscapes and rites of passage. I first encountered it, in all its essential bristliness, on Berkhamsted's common when I was at school. We were sent there on cross-country runs for punishments or when the weather was too wet for sport, along a mud path euphemistically known as the Broad Track. I loathed these plods on which I was wracked with stitch and ripped by whole tribes of thorny upstarts.

The gorse showed no favouritism. Barnes, a long-distance champion and heroic figure in the school, came back from a record-breaking run one afternoon with his legs covered in big weeping blisters. The school doctor diagnosed scratching by 'an infected gorse bush'. I reckoned *every* bush was toxic, and had no notion then that the great botanist Carl Linnaeus had apparently fallen to his knees on our common at the sight of a whole landscape blazing yellow.

But 'the old heath smells' that the poet George Meredith rhapsodised over must have got under my skin too, and by my twenties I'd fallen in love with the place and begun to learn a little of its history. The gorse had once been a crucial resource for the local commoners, as cattle fodder and fuel, especially for bread ovens. There was a sustainable and socially equitable code for cutting that was way ahead of its time. In 1725 the Manor Court specified the size and type of the cutting weapon. On pain of a five shilling fine, no person could cut gorse (called furze in this document) with any other weapon 'than a one-handed Bille with a stale helve or handle thereto affixed of the length of twelve inches.' One year later the order was amended to make exceptions for those over sixty and under fourteen, and for the disabled, who might use 'Hows or handbills but not longbills'.

A century later all this ancient etiquette was threatened when the lord of the manor, Lord Brownlow, tried to illegally enclose the common. This led to the historic Battle of Berkhamsted Common. On 6 March, 1866 (the gorse would have been in bloom), 120 hired London navvies took the train from Euston, marched to the common by moonlight and took down four miles of iron railings. The news spread fast, and the next day a press report told of how 'the inhabitants of the adjacent village and district flocked to the scene. In carriages, gigs, dogcarts, and on foot, gentry, shopkeepers, husbandmen, women and children, at once tested the reality of what they saw by strolling over and squatting on the Common and taking away morsels of gorse to prove, as they said, that the place was their own again.' Every time I read this report and imagine my ancestral townspeople claiming their commonplace talismans, I'm done for.

When I first moved from Berkhamsted to East Anglia I lived for a while on the edge of another sizeable common, Wortham Ling. Huge arching gorse bushes dominated the scene there too. The smaller ones were browsed by rabbits, and the patterns in which they nibbled, leaving little tufts at the top beyond their reach, sometimes created comic self-portraits. A little later I spent writing time at the Eden Project in Cornwall. The quarry in which the biomes sit was rimmed with gorse, a wild halo around this epicentre of cultivation. Then one day I spotted a bush that had insinuated itself inside the Humid Tropics Biome, a traveller across categories that seemed to suggest all kinds of possible vegetal futures.

On a Suffolk heath one June day, I was lying on my back under sprays of gorse blossom. The scent was tropical, with vanilla and melon there as well as coconut. Out of the blue I was hit by an extra burst of scent, that seemed to fill not just my nose but my eyes and cheeks. A few minutes later it happened again, and I wondered if it was an olfactory illusion, a momentary heightening of attention. Some change in me, not the plant. Then I wondered if the gorse might be rationing its costly scent molecules, emitting specially concentrated puffs as come-ons to insects. But I was struck by a more outlandish thought. Was the gorse smelling *me*, and responding to the presence of a large breathing organism? It was an immodest idea, but it led me to understand that plants receive scents as well as emit them, that they can decode the volatile chemicals emitted by insects and by other plants, and even respond to the scented breath of grazing animals.

Our own gorse patch is now the size of a small summerhouse. When it's in fullest flower in May, it's the most luminous spot in the garden. I await a stonechat dropping in and perching on what is one of its species' favourite shrubs, and making its clacking calls that echo the sound of gorse seed pods bursting open. What we get is more modest, but still thrumming with life: swarms of bumble bees and the ethereal webs of gorse spider-mites, like tents spun out of mist.

Like all old gorse bushes, it's now beginning to collapse. Its branches are straggling sideways, separating like a bunch of spillikins. And they've revealed something of which I had no inkling. Inside the tangled mass of dried pods and green spines three ashes, one oak and a cherry tree have sprung up, and are already as high as my shoulders. They've grown under the protection of the gorse just as young trees do in wild woods like the New Forest.

I've no idea if the ashes are the offspring of our own trees, or drifted in as keys from elsewhere, but they're a glimmer of hope for the future.

Our other gorse bush hangs above the hearth in our living room. It's a painting by the Cornish artist Kurt Jackson, and its mass of flowers glow like a fireball. Below them is a tangle of sticks and spines, scratched out with brush stubs (and maybe a gorse twig) and looking like some electric circuitry that powers the entire system. To one side a whole stem has slewed away, carrying its blooms like a torch on a bonfire night procession. And something uncanny I only spotted when I looked at the piece very closely: emerging from the top of the bush is what looks like the sprig of a young ash tree ... This is no pastoral portrait, a splodge of inert mustard on the side of a distant hill. This is a smouldering pyrotechnic, about to erupt with seed-burst and spine-stab and which you are very close to being *inside*.

I first met Kurt in the early 2000s, when he invited me to write the catalogue note for an exhibition on 'Ponds, Pools and Puddles'. It was the first time I'd encountered his paintings, and they were a revelation. He turns most of the conventions of landscape painting on their head – or more accurately back to front. Conventional perspective is rare. He looks *through* vegetation, *up* from hedge bottoms. When, more conventionally, he regards a whole scene, his low viewpoint and the sense of constant activity in his subject collapses the traditional sense that the painter *commands* the view, that he is at its focal point. Kurt's scenes seem to flow towards you. He calls his ponds and pools 'holes in the earth ... entrances into the unknown'. His 'Pool in woodland of ivy and sallow' shows just such a place; a dark and occult plane the colour of pewter, latticed over with branches – and with the reflections of branches. It makes me think of my own childhood pond-dipping, and the thrilling realisation that there was life beyond the surface of things. Glimpses of metamorphosis and, beyond simple reflections, of ourselves: some damp cryptic place like this was where life on Earth began. His pictures remind me of our own pond, with its ivy-scaling moorhens. That also feels like a portal: between wood and water, past and present, the ethereal and the physical.

I did more catalogue notes for Kurt, for collections on woods and orchards and edgelands, and found him a kindred spirit in his feeling for the dynamism and mischievousness of nature. He once said to me, 'I don't do pretty'. His work explores the inner energy of vegetation and landscape, how it works over how it looks. He read zoology at Oxford, but spent more time drawing the Thameside water meadows. He has the instincts and observational focus of a field naturalist and he paints much as his subjects live, riding the currents of opportunity and chance. He slaps on paint with broad brushes or his fingers, scribbles lines with sticks, accepts dust and debris flecks that are blowing about. On the wall in our living room opposite his gorse painting there's an artist's proof of a large charcoal and grey paint sketch of a Cornish wood in winter. Kurt is inside the wood looking out, and the fretwork of branches is splintering the low light. Here and there rain splashes leach the dark pigments into amorphous clouds.

Skewjack is the most south-westerly patch of wild wood-land in Britain, and maybe named from the Cornish word *skewyek*, for 'sheltered'. But it's the wind coming out of the picture that hits you. The spaces between the branches are a turmoil of twigs and leaves, all headed your way.

10

AFTERMATH

Winter in the garden is the season of the un-green. Everywhere pallid colours mark out stems and stones and crusty growths. In the Mediterranean garden, the Phlomis stalks ringed by whorls of dried-out flowers look as if they have been turned on a lathe. The wood is strewn with the moist open shells of conkers, like beached molluscs, their nuts munched away by deer. A carpet of twigs in taupe and khaki has been blown down by the wind. I find a hazel branch wrapped in a fungus that looks exactly like chewing gum. It's called Hazel Bracket, but I prefer the tongue-twisting scientific tag *Skeletocutis nivea*, which roughly translates as 'white withered skin'. Other windfall branches – some dropped like daggers into the ground – are wreathed in lichens, encrustations in grey and slate and lemon. I'm at the edge of my identification skills here, but I can recognise a few of the commoner ones. *Parmelia saxatilis*, a shield lichen, named from the shape and colour of its foliate outgrowths (from the root *parma* meaning shield); and *Physcia adscendens* whose grey sprouts turn tubular at their tips (*physcia* comes from a root meaning inflated). John Clare called lichens 'winter's foliage', and would have been gratified by what is now known about them. They were once thought to be simple partnerships between a green photosynthesising algae and a fungal shell. Now it's been found that many other fungal and bacterial species can be part of what is a complex symbiotic community. Two of our tree lichens are growing on my car, on a damp patch just under the headlight washing nozzle. I admire their opportunism, and wonder how their nomadic existence fits with my nostrums about plants and place.

I don't relish winter. Plant metabolism all but stops below about 8 degrees C, and I think mine does too. The cold makes my tissues stiffen. The low light levels sap my energy. I get bad-tempered and scowly. Thomas Hardy wrote that 'Cold weather brings out upon the faces of people the written marks of their habits, vices, passions and memories, as warmth brings out on a paper a writing in sympathetic ink.' On better days Polly's grandchildren come over and animate us, drawn here by food and fire. In mid autumn they enact the *vendage*, the grape harvest. Our vine's an unruly growth, inextricably entwined with a climbing rose on a pergola in the gravel. Their combined foliage is so matted that it keeps the rain off if we are eating underneath. The grapes are small, prolific and bitter-sweet and we gather what the blackbirds have left us to make into juice. The kids form an assembly line, picking, stripping, sorting, cranking through a *moulin*, pouring juice into bottles, or themselves. Later they like a cook-up in the wood, on a brazier fashioned from the drum of an old washing machine. They make what I used to call twists, and Polly's family call dampers, ribbons of unleavened dough wrapped round a peeled stick and held over the embers. The kids stoop and twirl their sticks, sometimes maddened by impatience and pushing them into the flames instead. Then dousing their half-baked concoctions in golden syrup. The end results often resemble the corner of a Kurt Jackson painting, a collage of mud-smears and bits of leaf.

At this early evening time, our neighbourhood jackdaws come to roost in the trees, deep in their comforting chatter, a performance of extraordinary affective contrasts – quiet mutterings, excited xylophone ripples and long polyphonic passages that suggest a serious discussion about the day's events. But most of the local farmland birds aren't at peace. The flocks of golden plover and lapwing that wintered in the fields outside the garden when we first moved in have disappeared. So have the barn owls I always used to see on late afternoon pootles. There were a dozen territories within five miles. I don't know if they've deserted us, deprived of hunting habitats, or just vanished into the greater security of the night. A 2023 study by the National Academy of Sciences reports that half a billion birds of 170 species have vanished from Europe over the past forty years, chiefly as a result of intensive chemical agriculture.

So, when the ice-ups finally arrive I take no pleasure in the crystal structures of hoar frost. It's the starved barn owls I think of, the wrens frozen in porches, the hundreds of dying redwings I once found on a Norfolk beach, caught in an ice storm over the North Sea. A doctor remarked of my glum winter moods, 'It's not seasonal depression, laddie. You just don't like what's out there.'

By mid December I've had enough, and begin to count the days till spring. But then up pops St Lucy's Eve, 13 December, a day of ends and beginnings, which John Donne described in his 'Nocturnal' as 'the year's midnight … The world's whole sap is sunk'. St Lucy, because her name shares the root of the Greek word *lux* (and because she was blinded during her martyrdom) has always been the saint of light. Her appointed day was originally on the winter solstice, the shortest day, the cusp between dark and light. In the muddled and inconsistent Julian calendar this used to fall on 13 December, give or take a couple of days. In 1752 the calendar was revised to accord with the more accurate Gregorian version. This meant the subtraction of eleven whole days from that first year, so that the solstice now falls between 20 and 22 December. But because of the asymmetry of the Earth's orbit, the evenings and mornings don't begin lightening evenly on either side of the solstice. The latest sunrise is around ten days after the shortest day, the earliest sunset around ten days before. So St Lucy's Day may be the 'year's midnight' but it's also a kind of crepuscular dawn, the occasion when the evenings, as my mum used to put it, begin to 'draw out'. A small chink in winter's curtain opens, and we celebrate, as they do in Scandinavia, with candles and saffron buns. I find it absurdly heartening to see in the almanack that in seven days' time the sun will be setting all of one minute later.

This slightly liturgical mood lingers, and on dismal Sunday afternoons we often desert the garden and go church crawling. East Anglia's ancient churches are a treasure house. I'm still hazy about the finer points of ecclesiastical architecture, but I'm fascinated by its natural iconography, and the portal it gives to the mindsets of the medievals. I sense that they were as ambivalent about nature as us, seeing it at once as fearful, neighbourly, absurd. Images of wildmen – 'wodewoses', scaly or simian – abound in our churches, often alongside Trees of Life or lions guarding the angels on the font. Misericords and screens have casts of figures that seem to have come out of Aesop's fables – a rabbit caught by its hind-legs, a fox with a goose in its jaws. The local landscape leaks into the church, and is as likely to become a cartoon as a metaphor, just as the gargoyles are often caricatures of local bigwigs. In what were once called the Dark Ages, nature was seen by some church elders as an extension of the flesh, the accursed habitat of sin. The influential eighth-century theologian Rabanus Maurus regarded even images of leaves as standing for 'lustful or wicked men doomed to damnation'. Fortunately he was ignored by the stone carvers, and English churches are full of foliage and flowers: rose motifs, symbolic leaves, fleurons and naturalistic carvings of the plants that might well be growing in the churchyard – buttercups, wild strawberry, hops, ivy, oak, hawthorn. Over in the great wool churches of East Anglia's fenland there's a bestiary of what was then England's largest and wildest wetland. In the choir-stalls and pews there are fishes, swans, beavers, stags racing through the reeds, herons stabbing eels. In the air above are wooden angels, just taking off from the hammer beams. These aren't the angels of Renaissance paintings, with broad wings neatly folded. They're creatures in full flight, with long narrow wings and splayed feathers at the tips. I would be surprised if whoever carved these creatures hadn't been inspired by marsh harriers, then common birds in the fenland reed beds, and whose springtime sky-dancing must have seemed to have something numinous about it.

I'm reminded of Palaeolithic cave paintings by these vernacular artworks. They have the same relish in the energy of life, the same sharply observed detail. They can be comic, reverent, sometimes subversive, but are rooted in real lives lived alongside ours. The magnificent flying angels in Suffolk's Blythburgh church are riddled with shot-holes, and for a long time these were believed to have come from the guns of Oliver Cromwell's iconoclasts on their hunt for idolatrous flights of fancy. When the pellets were finally found and identified, they turned out to date from two centuries later. The churchwardens had been shooting jackdaws, not angels.

It's late July again, the first anniversary of the great heatwave, and close to the twentieth anniversary of our Beating of the Bounds. It's a mild day, and our normally secretive chiffchaff has taken to singing from the top of the television aerial. I envy his panoramic view of our garden and decide to walk the course again for old time's sake. The pond is low and as cryptic as ever, the ash trees still healthy. Turkey oak seedlings are sprouting along the edge of the wood, among knapweeds and mallow spread from the meadow. My Med bed has survived the rigours of another English winter. Its limestone pathways are not as open and convincingly Cretan as they were, but at least what's smothering them are pillows of everlasting pea from southern France, in three shades of pink. And surfacing through the myrtle bush is something that makes me smile with delight and disbelief. Earlier in the summer a common mullein was growing on this spot. And as invariably happens, it was entirely demolished by the caterpillars of mullein shark moths, whose polka-dot coats in black and yellow are as striking as their voracious appetites. But now it's regrown, with a stem as fat and hoary as an old cabbage, and bearing a candelabra of flowers just like its cousins on the A47. It's supporting sprays of hedgerow cranesbill and new euphorbia seedlings and looking like a vignette of the entire garden project.

The weather all over Britain these past six months has seen bizarre alternations and unseasonable extremes. Every month seemed to break some record. February was the driest for thirty years, March the wettest for forty years. April's brief spells of fine weather saw spectacular displays of blossom, until an abrupt change in May to cold and wind made pollination erratic. The pears failed and our wild cherries set minute quantities of fruit (so no clafoutis this year). Polly's root vegetables struggled to germinate. Pigeons stripped the lettuce seedlings, and we continued our debate about vegetable-growing's future being likely to lie indoors. Meanwhile, the impeccably native subterranean honey fungus, with its special liking for all rose family species, inched forward (it's creeping south at about one metre a year) and claimed our *Rosa mutabilis*.

June was the hottest on record, July the sixth wettest. In the world beyond, global heating is generating scenarios far more devastating. Floods and massive wildfires have erupted across the Mediterranean, Hawaii, Australia, California, Canada. Climate scientists reckon that globally the summer is the hottest for 120,000 years. I am weirdly nagged by memories of Shakespeare's *A Midsummer Night's Dream*, written in the late 1590s, during an acute period of the climate upheavals of the Little Ice Age. In the play there is unnatural weather in the forest, and the queen of the fairies, Titania, blames it all on her spouse Oberon's acquisitiveness: 'Contagious fogs, which falling on the land, / Hath every pelting river made so proud / That they have overborne their continents ... And through this distemperature we see / The seasons alter: hoary-headed frosts / Fall in the fresh lap of the crimson rose'. Seeking revenge on his queen, Oberon orders his familiar, Puck, to fetch him that 'little western flower', the juice of which, when dropped on Titania's eyes as she slept, would make her 'madly dote / Upon the next live creature that [she] sees'. The magical properties are invented of course, all part of Shakespeare's playmaking mischief. But the flower itself is real, and cannily chosen. It's the little wild pansy widely known as heartsease, and in the Midlands as love-in-idleness, a name tailored for the amorous agonies acted out in the midsummer forest.

And then something odd happened. In the early

summer a tiny specimen of this plant sprung up in a patch of short grass that edged the gravel. It was a deep rich, blue-violet with a sparkling yellow eye, and a mysterious arrival. It grows here and there in sandy fields in Norfolk, but I have never found it within twenty kilometres of our house and I have no idea how it came to be here.

Now, in late July, everything in the garden seems to be cast under a spell. The sun has briefly returned and brought about a transformation worthy of the *Dream's* dramas of reconciliation and repair. Some alchemy wrought by the successions of heat and wet has produced an unprecedented profusion of growth and hatching and migration, and I'm madly doting on it all. Courgettes and beans suddenly choke the vegetable garden. The hawthorns are so densely cloaked with tawny fruit they look prematurely autumnal. Blackberries are already ripening, and Polly is pulling them off the bushes as if she were milking them. The grass in the meadow is now taller than me. Paths and doors are festooned with vegetation, and we will have to cut some human-shaped holes soon. The moorhens have produced two striped leucistic chicks, which stalk the garden like small clockwork magpies. A turtle dove, now one of Britain's rarest summer visitors, arrives in our wood, and despite the lateness of the season begins to sing, that drowsy, hypnotic purr that has enchanted our species as far back as the Song of Solomon. I think achingly of France, the last place I heard one, and then, rather ashamed of myself, give thanks we have one here.

But it's the butterflies which have changed the whole complexion of the garden. Confounding the Jeremiahs who'd predicted their decimation as a result of last year's summer heat, they mob us in their hundreds: clouds of whites, browns, late brood brimstones, red admirals up from southern Europe. In places, especially by tufts of marjoram, it's hard to walk without them fluttering against your face. On one day we count thirteen different species flying. They're joined by hummingbird hawk-moths, which this year are nectaring very sedately on the everlasting pea as well as frenetically on the valerian. And two hornet-mimic hoverflies, burnished with brassy stripes, are feeding on the mint flowers. Thoroughly vege-tarian animals, unlike their namesakes, they evolved under a false flag for safety. They're from mainland Europe, and weren't spotted in Britain until the 1940s, since when they've spread through south and eastern England.

Why this great incursion of southern organisms? Global heating and, this summer, Mediterranean super-heating, is almost certainly the cause, as it is behind the new breeding birds of Norfolk: bee-eaters nesting on the coast and the increasing numbers of great white and cattle egrets we see on the Broads, all settlers from the Medi-terranean. We are rightly told to see these newcomers as warning signs of the dramatic ecological changes under-way. But it's wrong to compare them, as they have been, to 'miners' canaries'. The point about the canaries was that they were gassed in their cages, mortal victims of a polluted environment. These migrant species have used their mobility to escape to more clement conditions, and we have a duty to welcome them. They are like Hiroshi-ma's *hibakujumoku* trees, survivors, emblems of hope.

★

Looking at our two acres now, twenty years after we moved in, I see something that might be called a fusion garden. Native plants and animals form new communities with benign immigrant species. Turkey oaks grow through the English cherries, the Painted Lady sits on the Drunken Sailor, the south-east Asian deer browses a wilding rose whose ancestors may stretch across two continents. The minor victories in a garden aren't any answer to our global crises. The worldwide collapse of biodiversity is as great a threat to the planet as climate change, and much less addressed. And beyond the self-interest and inertia of governments and big business there are wider cultural blocks to this. We still, as a species, are largely wedded to two ingrained ideas: human privilege and nature's dependency. I like to think that in our accidental garden we've had a glimpse of the fallacy – and I'd suggest, the dubious ethics – of these dogmas. Even small refuges and enclaves where natural processes are encouraged seem able to make a stand, however brief, against the tides of loss and degradation. Maybe a willingness to learn from the adaptations and solutions of life systems that have been coping with adversity for 3.7 billion years should be added to our coping strategies.

But what of the gardener, without whose presence the concept of 'a garden' is meaningless. I try my best to stay in my earthworm mode: low profile, minimum intervention. But I'm human, and as Lewis Thomas reminds us, a member of 'this kind of species': meddlers, makers, experimenters. So my stick, life's first tool, still waves and points and prods and bashes, maybe doing things that are more rewarding for me than for the garden's other inhabitants. But I keep in mind the frankly absurd privilege of owning a patch of planet Earth, and try to pay my dues. We can play other roles beyond the planning and planting and pruning, roles that are also special to our human identity. Be interpreters, scribes, witnesses, neighbours. The welcomers at the gate.

ACKNOWLEDGEMENTS

Working on this short book has been an outing with old friends, and I thank all those pals who have contributed their pennyworth: Brett Westwood, Bob Gibbons, James Robertson, Robin and Rachel Hamilton for their ecological wisdom. James Canton for his own splendidly wild patch. The late Ronald Blythe for his shining respect for his garden neighbours and his unforgettable plot at Bottengoms. Mark Cocker for his suggestions about structure. Kurt Jackson for his friendship and immersive paintings. My gratitude to Rick Rickord for crafting my swagger stick, and to Ray Reynolds and his team for the heavier work in the garden, and for so enthusiastically embracing what must have seemed at first like wildly eccentric ambitions. Jon Cook and Alexandra Harris read early drafts and gave advice and support without which the text would not only have been incoherent but probably never even finished. At Profile, Andrew Franklin was, as ever, a pillar of support. Penny Daniel, my editor, swept away contradictions, obscurities and extravagances while always recognising the core of what I was trying to say. Penny Gardiner was scrupulous in her copyediting, especially with the niceties

of botanical jargon. Thanks to Steve Coventry-Panton for
the beautiful jacket, including a special thank you to Tessa
Newcomb, whose watercolour of a lone blackbird on top
of an allotment bean pole served as inspiration.

Finally, my heartfelt love and thanks to Polly, my and
the garden's even keel. She grows our food, keeps the
basic structure of the plot intact, and keeps the structure
of my life intact too, through the frets and follies of this
writing game. This book is dedicated to her.

NOTES

p. 1 *most commodious of institutions*: R. S. Thomas, (1913–2000). From his poem 'The Garden', in *The Bread of Truth* (Rupert Hart-Davis, 1963)

p. 3 *Happily we shared*: Gerard Manley Hopkins (1844–89). From his poem 'Inversnaid'.

p. 4 *a similarly ancient farmhouse*: Ronald Blythe, *Next to Nature* (John Murray, 2022)

p. 5 *biologist and essayist*: Lewis Thomas, 'The Wonderful Mistake', in *The Medusa and the Snail* (Viking Press, 1979)

p. 14 *nicknamed the Sandwalk*: Darwin's Sandwalk, see Adrian Desmond and James Moore, *Darwin*, (Penguin, 1992)

p. 16 *examine the nature:* Gilbert White's *Journals*, ed. Francesca Greenoak (Century Hutchinson Ltd, 1986–9)

p. 22 *a centre of the hemp growing*: Hemp cultivation. See Eric Pursehouse, *Waveney Valley Studies* (Diss Publishing Co Ltd, 1966)

p. 25 *a sneaking admiration*: John Evelyn. *Acetaria, A Discourse of Sallets*, 1699. *Fumifugium, or The Inconvenience of the Aer and Smoke of London Dissipated*, 1661. *Sylva, or a Discourse of Forest Trees*, 1664. For an account of Evelyn's garden see: Mark Laird, *A Natural History of English Gardening: 1650–1800* (Yale University Press, 2015)

p. 26 *the ambivalent character of fertility*: Marvell. Nigel Smith (ed), *The Poems of Andrew Marvell* (Longman, 2006)

p. 26 *vegetal autonomy* :William Robinson's life. Mea Allen, *William Robinson, 1838–1935. Father of the English Flower Garden*, (Faber & Faber, 1982). Robinson, *The Wild Garden*, 1870 (extended edition with Rick Darke: Timber Press, 2010)

p. 30 *the most complex word*: Raymond Williams, *Keywords. A Vocabulary of Culture and Society* (Croom Helm, 1976)

p. 35 *the impact of photography*: 'The Work of Art in the Age of Mechanical Reproduction', Walter Benjamin, *Illuminations* (Jonathan Cape, 1970)

p. 37 *making tentative enclosure incursions*: Roydon Riots. See Pursehouse, op cit.

p. 45 *are small and distinctive*: Yellow-rattle. C. C. Gibson and A. R.Watkinson, 'The host range and selectivity of a parasitic plant, *Rhinanthus minor L'*, *Oecologia*, vol. 78 no. 3 (1989), pp. 401–406

p. 47 *the meadows at Appleton House*: Marvell. Nigel Smith, op cit.

p. 50 *alights on the lip*: M. J. Godfery, *British Orchidaceae* (Cambridge University Press, 1933)

p. 53 *et in arcadia ego*: Literally, 'Even in Arcadia I am there' – 'I' being death. A tomb with this inscription amid a pastoral setting is first mentioned in Virgil's *Eclogues*

p. 63 *Our ideal wood*: From Richard Mabey and Tony Evans, *The Flowering of Britain* (Hutchinson, 1980)

p. 63 *Dorset copses he knew as a child*: Extract from 'Woods', by Louis MacNeice, in *Collected Poems* (Faber & Faber, 1991), © The estate of Louis MacNeice

p. 65 *a key location in his novel*: John Fowles, foreword to Elaine Franks, *The Undercliff* (J. M. Dent and Sons, 1989)

Notes

p. 66 *a wood of my own*: Story in Richard Mabey,
  Beechcombings (Chatto and Windus, 2007)

p. 70 *'present naturalness'*: George Peterken, *Natural Woodland*
  (Cambridge University Press, 1996)

p. 72 *'Hooper's Law'*: Max Hooper with N. Moore and E.
  Pollard, *Hedges* (Collins, 1974)

p. 74 *a single parish treeland*: Henry Thoreau, 'Walking' or
  'The Wild', lecture first published as an essay in *Atlantic
  Monthly*, 1862

p. 77 *once described scrub as*: Nan Fairbrother, *New Lives, New
  Landscapes* (Architectural Press, 1970)

p. 83 *the serpentine limb:* Mabey, *Beechcombings,* op cit.

p. 83 *internal negotiation in oak*: John Ruskin, *Modern Painters,
  Volume 5. Of Leaf Beauty* (G. Routledge, 1860)

p. 84 *the state of transcendental calm*: James Canton, *The Oak
  Papers* (Canongate Books, 2020)

p. 85 *I don't see much distinction:* Mark Cocker, review of Ed
  Yong, *An Immense World*, *New Statesman*, 8 July 2022

p. 86 *Turkey oaks were introduce*d: See Ben Rose, 'The Spread
  of Turkey Oak in the British Isles', *British Wildlife*, Feb
  2017

p. 90 *We tend to think of weeds*: Richard Mabey, *Weeds* (Profile
  Books, 2010)

p. 94 *housebound by chronic illness*: John Keats, Letter to
  Reynolds, in Robert Gittings, *John Keats* (Little, Brown,
  1968)

p. 97 *My first book: Food for Free* (Collins, 1972)

p. 98 *'Shadows of Taste':* in John Clare, *The Midsummer
  Cushion*, ed Anne Tibble (Carcanet Press for Mid
  Northumberland Arts Group, 1978)

p. 99 *In his meditation*: John Fowles, *The Tree* (Little Toller
  Books, 1979)

p. 100 *'a form of permanent geography'*: Ronald Blythe, 'An Inherited Perspective', in *From the Headlands* (Chatto & Windus, 1982)

p. 100 *popular botanical field-guides*: Reverend W. Keble Martin et al, *Flora of Devon* (T. Buncle & Co. Ltd, 1939)

p. 100 *plants in the exact locations*: Gilbert White, *Journals*, op cit.

p. 104 *arguments about the provenance*: Richard Mabey, *Flora Britannica* (Chatto & Windus / Sinclair Stevenson, 1996)

p. 104 *in a Suffolk meadow*: Geoffrey Grigson, *The Englishman's Flora* (Phoenix House, 1955)

p. 105 *mentions it in his* Herball: John Gerard, *The Herball, or General Historie of Plantes* (John Norton, 1597)

p. 105 *long-established natives*: Peter Marren, 'How important is native status? Conservation and "alien" plants'. *British Wildlife,* August 2019

p. 108 *'Going abroad'*: Geoffrey Grigson, *A Herbal of All Sorts* (Phoenix House, 1959)

p. 119 *I walk around such gardens:* Geoffrey Grigson, 'The Unnatural Garden', *Gardenage* (Routledge Kegan Paul, 1952)

p. 119 *'It needed "Improvement"'*: See 'In a Brown Shade', in Richard Mabey, *Turning the Boat for Home* (Chatto & Windus, 2019)

p. 120 *Mediterranean cave art*: Guillaume Desanges, catalogue note for Duprat

p. 122 *proportions of the water plantain*: Ruskin's theory of beauty, see Peter Fuller, *Theoria. Art and the Absence of Grace* (Chatto & Windus, 1988)

p. 130 *a favourite epithet*: William Robinson, *The Wild Garden*, op cit.

Notes

p. 132 '...*The Dunwich Rose*': quoted in William Dutt, *Highways and Byways of East Anglia* (Macmillan, 1901)

p. 139 *'the old heath smells'*: George Meredith, from his poem 'Juggling Jerry', Reprinted in *Modern Love, and Poems of the English Roadside, with poems and ballads* (Chapman and Hall, 1859)

p. 139 *ancient etiquette was threatened*: Berkhamsted Common. See George H. Whybrow, *The History of Berkhamsted Common* (Commons, Open Spaces and Footpaths Preservation Society, 1934)

p. 146 *'Cold weather brings out'*: *Thomas Hardy's Notebooks*, ed. Evelyn Hardy (St Martin's Press, 1955)

p. 147 *A 2023 study*: 'Farmland practices are driving bird population decline across Europe', *Proceedings of the National Academy of Sciences* (University of Michigan, 2023)